- "The FAPA President's Book Award exists to promote excellence in the publishing industry by recognizing talented contemporary authors who put both heart and soul into their work. FAPA is proud to be a champion of authors and publishers going the extra mile to produce books of excellence in every aspect." said *Jane R. Wood, President-Elect of FAPA.*

- "We are proud to announce this year's winner *Robert Hogg, Jr.* who truly embody the excellence this award was created to celebrate. We had a record number of entries this year. Competition was stiff! We salute all of our writers for their fine work," said *FAPA's President, Terri Gerrell.*

2017 FAPA PRESIDENT'S BOOK AWARD WINNER
2X SILVER METALLIST

The UNTOLD Story

PREPARATION FOR LIFE AFTER A SPORTS CAREER

ROBERT HOGG, JR.
WITH **LOUIS GOGGANS**

©2015 Robert Hogg, Jr. with Louis Goggans
All rights reserved

Library of Congress Control Number:
2016930798

ISBN 978-0-9837566-6-8

No part of this book may be reproduced, stored in a retrieval system, or transmitted in any form or by any means, electronic, mechanical, photocopying, recording or otherwise without the written permission of the author.

Published by
Emerge Publishing Group, LLC
Riviera Beach, FL
www.emergepublishers.com

Robert Hogg, Jr. with Louis Goggans, 2015
"The Untold Story: Preparation for Life After a Sports Career"
1. Autobiographical. 2. Inspirational.

Printed in the United States of America

CONTENTS

Author's Message viii

Louis Goggans x

Preface xi

PART I - Life Lessons of Robert Hogg Jr.

The Beginning 3

Building the Foundation 7

First Love 11

The Journey 13

Game Week 17

Brownsville Road Broncos 19

New Beginnings 21

Making a Name for Myself 23

PART II - College

The System 33

Numbers Don't Lie 43

CONTENTS (CONT'D)

PART III -

Athlete to Athlete	47
Jeremy Kellem	49
Coty Senesabaugh	53
Samuel Seamster	57
Vince Carter	69
Mike Conley	71
Robert Hogg, Jr.	73
France Makabu	89
Leslie Cikra	93
Angel Cassandra Nathan	107
Mori Taheripour	111
Teddy Gaines	123

PART IV -

My Advice to Student Athletes	139
Take Control of your Life	147

Dedication

This book is dedicated:
To my father Robert Sr.,
To my mother Charlene,
To my sister Rasheeda, and
To anyone who has ever believed in me.
And to those damn off season workouts that made you contemplate about Life.

ROBERT HOGG, JR.

SPECIAL THANK YOU TO
Contributing Athletes, Athletic Personnel, Personnel in Athlete Development:

Jeremy Kellem, Coty Senesabaugh, Samuel Seamster, Vince Carter, Mike Conley, France Makabu, Leslie Cikra, Angel Cassandra Nathan, Mori Taheripour, Teddy Gaines

ROBERT HOGG, JR.

Author's Message

Dear Reader,

I have encountered various set-backs in my life that have molded me into the man that I have become today. The majority of set-backs are due to my ignorance or lack of knowledge in a particular area. In life there are many signs that you encounter on the road of your life journey. It is wise to take time and observe your whereabouts from time to time to understand where you are going. If you are lost and continue going forward you will probably end up on a road that leads to a dead end.

Through my mistakes and set-backs I hope for you to find the good in it, and use my experiences as a learning lesson to bring good fortune to yourself and your family. Life is all about learning and getting better over time. Emptying my cup of blessings, to you the reader, will enlighten you to *The Untold Story* of a student athlete career journey. You are welcome in advance.

Robert Hogg, Jr.
Author

ROBERT HOGG, JR.

Louis Goggans

Louis Goggans is an Alabama-born, Tennessee-bred award-winning journalist. Possessing an immense passion for storytelling, Goggans has been writing since a youth. He earned his Bachelor of Arts in Journalism from the University of Memphis (U of M). He wrote for the school's newspaper, The Daily Helmsman, and also served as president of the U of M's Association of Black Journalists.

In 2011, Goggans became a staff reporter for the Memphis Flyer, an alternative weekly newspaper based in Memphis, TN. Over his four-year tenure with the publication, he covered an array of topics including crime, health, education, nonprofit agencies, paternity fraud, poverty, and music.

In 2014, Goggans won awards in the investigative reporting category at the 64th Annual Green Eyeshade Awards (the nation's oldest regional journalism contest) for his feature articles on the unsolved murder of former NBA star Lorenzen Wright and human trafficking in the Mid-South.

This year, for the 65th Annual Green Eyeshade Awards, Goggans won awards for his features on Memphis' subtle but alarming HIV/AIDS rates and the Mid-South's prescription drug use epidemic.

Goggans currently serves as the Community Outreach Specialist/Public Information Officer for the U.S. Attorney's Office, Western District of Tennessee.

ROBERT HOGG, JR.

Preface

Welcome to the Real World

On December 1st, 2012 I found myself defeated! Not just any other loss, but the one that's demoralizing. It was one of those losses that you can only shrug your shoulders and shake your head. Not only did I lose a conference championship game, but my collegiate football career was over. A 22-year-old at the time, I was at a crossroads in my life. On that day, my alma mater Middle Tennessee State University played Arkansas State University in the Sun Belt Conference Championship. The situation was simple: Win and become conference champions and move on to a bowl game, or lose and still be bowl eligible, but your fate lies in the hands of a bowl committee. Whelp! We lost 45-0. Got routed. Pretty much didn't show up.

In retrospect, I went from potentially being a Sun Belt Conference Champion, bowl game participant, and receiving my Bachelor of Science in Construction Management to a recent graduate with a degree and an obsolete football career. This all happened in a matter of 14 days. My senior season had come to an abrupt end: We got snubbed on a bowl bid because of a business decision the university and conference committees had agreed upon. At the moment, I was bitter of the way my football career ended. During my senior season, my team was projected to finish second to last, and nobody expected anything from us. Nevertheless, we finished second in our conference, which speaks volumes of my senior season. As I reflect on my last semester as an undergraduate, everything went by so fast; it was a blur. In spite of things not going the way I desired, I have no regrets. But I do wish I finished both the season and semester better, or at least rode off in the sunset as a winner instead of experiencing a humiliating defeat.

I went from a student-athlete who was potentially bowl-bound to a recent graduate with no real world work experience. This was very tough, and it showed me how harsh life can be when you're not prepared. I learned everything is earned in life, nothing is given. After I graduated, I still had a desire to play football, but I was unsure of my chances to play professionally because I lacked prototypical size and quality film to validate my athletic ability. Instead of being picked up by a team, I was picked up by a car manufacturing company: Johnson Controls Inc. (JCI). I worked there to make ends meet while I trained for my pro-day and other professional try-outs. However, like the famous saying goes, "Things don't always go the way that you planned."

It was the second Saturday in May. I was just coming from my fourth and final Canadian Football League (CFL) tryout for the Edmonton Eskimos in Cincinnati, Ohio. I was thinking, 'If my agent or I don't hear back from any organizations by August, I'm going to move on with my life and put football in the past.' That's exactly what happened: No calls, minimum interest, and I did not want to play in a league that lacked efficient benefits for participating organizations.

My plan to leave JCI after three months backfired. I was still working in the car manufacturing factory nine months after graduating from college. This rough period taught me a lot about patience, humility, and faith. Every day was a reality check; I learned a little more about life and the real world. As a student-athlete in college, you're relatively oblivious to the world around you. During that period of my life, it was always about preparation for the next assignment, exam, or game. But as a young man entering the work industry, I was at the bottom of the corporate ladder, just trying to make a living.

I would like to elaborate a little more on my experience working at JCI. First and foremost, it validated why it is important to have an education in today's society. Without education and a specialized skill, you're merely building someone else's dream. I worked in the car manufacturing industry for a year and four months. It was incredibly hard going to work when I was not motivated, not to mention I was overqualified for the position. I did not go to school to work in a factory. It seemed like my bosses only viewed employees as another face that contributed to an assembly. "If you quit today, we will have another face the next day to fill your spot."

My job at JCI was to assemble as many truck seats as possible, which would be shipped to the Nissan plant in Smyrna, TN every single day. After the first three months, I hated working in the factory. The individuals I would talk to had no goals, no dreams and didn't want anything out of life but the bare minimum. But I always tried to stay positive and optimistic, so I would not fall in the self-pity and no-direction mindset my peers possessed. Work slowly became something I despised. I would see my former collegiate peers getting great jobs in their field. This made me start to look at myself as if I were lacking potential or not as qualified as my peers. I turned in numerous resumes and had various interviews for positions in my field, but I didn't receive a follow-up call or any opportunity. This left me with one alternative: Make my dreams a reality by stepping out on faith and outside of my comfort zone.

ROBERT HOGG, JR.

PART I

Life Lessons of Robert Hogg Jr.

THE BEGINNING

Competition is one of the greatest assets an individual can utilize to determine the level of character, determination, and endurance they possess. 'So, what exactly is competition? Who am I competing against? Why am I competing?' These are several questions individuals should ask themselves if they want to be successful. Competition is the driving force of improving who you are on a consistent basis. Repeatedly, throughout my life I have heard, 'If you are not getting better, you are getting worse. There is no staying the same.' Self- motivation is one of the most vital skills to ever be blessed with. It's rewarding to have the ability to motivate yourself on a daily basis to outperform your previous achievements. Life is very difficult. Every day you have to embrace the mentality to learn what you did in the past, focus on the present, and plan for the future. Without a plan, along with the knowledge and burning desire to successfully execute it, you will continue to fail in the search of who you're destined to be.

Before I go any further, I would like to provide a little background on myself.

I was born in Memphis, Tennessee, a blue-collar place adversely impacted by crime, poverty, and hopelessness. The vital keys to survival for many are hard work and determination. I was the second child born to Dr. Robert Hogg, Sr. and Charlene Hogg. To this very day, I consider them both my heroes and role models. I have one sibling, my older sister, Rasheeda Hogg. She's also my best friend and has provided me with unwavering support over the years.

My father worked for the government, which was very demanding and required our family to move often. Despite having a demanding work schedule, he made time for me. Two valuable things he taught me, which I'm extremely grateful for, is work ethic and taking ownership of my life. My father was very proactive and keen about taking initiative. Observing him over the course of my life gave me a role model; I was able to see somebody do the right thing on a daily basis. No shortcuts, excuses, or procrastinating. And I had the opportunity to learn these principles first- hand. I can honestly say my accomplishments thus far would have been nonexistent if it wasn't for my father.

I consider my mother, Charlene, the backbone of the family. She's everything one could desire to find in a mother: smart, sophisticated, real, down-to-earth, and nurturing. If my father could not answer, or help whatever problem I had, my mother would surely point me in the right direction and assist me. She has taught me so many significant things through my journey of life that has made me the man I am. Two of the biggest has been the importance of having faith in the Lord, and planting a seed for today so that I can live off the harvest for tomorrow.

Rasheeda, my sister, is my only sibling and best friend. We are four years apart, and I am open to talk to her about anything that might concern me. We have such an open relationship. It's a blessing to have a sibling that you're close with and who can share valuable insight on life.

I have lived in several cities before the age of fourteen which are: Memphis, TN, Ashland, KY, London, KY, Lexington, KY, and Kingsport, TN. Moving from city to city at an early age was pretty tough. I was too young to understand the blessings that were ahead of me. All I could think of was losing the friends that I made, along with the burden of having to find more in a new city.

I missed out on the traditional childhood of starting school with close friends and being able to graduate high school together. However, my upbringing was very unique; instead of me having a restricted set of friends, I collected a diverse set of acquaintances from each area I resided in. As a child I could not understand how important this was; it enabled me to establish a network of resources that would, and continues to, provide me with opportunities. I was introduced to so many cultures that I would not have gotten the chance to meet if I had stayed in Memphis my whole life. As I matured, I realized how important it was to broaden my surroundings. It made me a diverse person, enabling me to interact with people from various walks of life — a quality that is extremely vital. I have heard the statement often, "It is not what you know; it is who you know". I consider this to be very true. You might have elite knowledge in a specialized area, but if you do not know the right people to be around, the likelihood of failure increases dramatically.

BUILDING THE FOUNDATION

It was spring of 1999. I was eight years old and had moved back to Memphis, TN from Lexington, KY. I had lived in Lexington for three years before moving back home. When I returned, I had no friends, just my family to hang around. My life was simple: I would go to school, play video games, and watch TV. I never gave too much thought about my future, I just knew I wanted to meet more kids and have fun. During the three years I lived in Lexington, I developed friendships and relationships with numerous kids. Rasheeda was about twelve years old at the time. She attended Shadowlawn Middle School, which was on the boundaries of Bartlett and Arlington. She started to meet friends at school and began to have fun unlike me. I would pretty much follow her around all day just so I would not be at home alone all the time, which I hated.

In Lexington, KY my sister ran track for Leestown Middle School. She also cheered for the school's basketball team. I remember always going to the games to watch her cheer; as well as going to her track meets with my father and thinking, "Wow, my big sis is pretty fast, and has a lot of pride." The first spring after we moved from Lexington, we started to seek track tryouts around the Raleigh/ Bartlett area in Memphis. The youth sports organization was called Shelby Youth Sports (SYS). Under the program, a collection of different areas of Memphis collaborated to make a five-to-seventeen-year-old program for each gender. SYS offered track and field, football, and cheerleading. My sister signed up instantly after seeing the fliers. I was actually terrified: I did not know anything about track and field or competing. I thought I was fast because I was usually picked first in all the games during recess, but I really didn't know my skill level in organized sports.

My memory of the beginning of my track career is very vivid. I remember intense track practices after elementary and middle school classes. And all of the passionate arguments at school with rival teams before track meets on Saturday. I started to develop the mentality that nothing is given, everything is earned. There are no hand-outs in this world. If it's easy to obtain, it holds no value, and you will probably lose it easily. Anything that you shed blood, sweat, and tears for has value in your life.

I can still remember the scorching Memphis heat that caused us to sweat profusely during afternoon track practices in the middle of spring. Fortunately, there was also a cooling wind that would keep practices bearable until the sun went down. At practice, we would run, run, and run some more. We would run so much that my body would be incredibly sore while I sat in class the following day.

My early track experience was humbling to say the least. We didn't have a track to run on for practice. Instead, we would run around the neighborhood of Brownsville Road Elementary or in the grass on the football field. We didn't have any state of the art facilities or the best coaches, but we did have pride, talent, and the desire to compete. I was a part of the Brownsville Road Broncos. I had a pretty successful career as a Broncos. Coach Joe Jones, Coach Rick Poston, and Coach Reginald Tooley, Sr were some of my very first coaches, and they instilled a lot of character in me.

Coach Jones and Poston had a military background and drilled some of their discipline and training into our team. Coach Tooley was a former college student athlete at Florida A&M University, where he played defensive back. He brought a very unique point of view to the game.

All of our coaches were all volunteers and worked full-time jobs. They would teach the team life lessons, which is more beneficial than wins or losses or any individual achievements for that matter.

FIRST LOVE

After track season ended and the blazing hot summer days in Memphis arrived, talk of football season began to be discussed by peers. Although it was a game that I enjoyed to watch, I was terrified at actually playing. Nevertheless, I decided to try it out. The closer the days got to the beginning of football camp, the more frightened I became. I had never tackled anyone; I had never played tackle football with anyone; and I had never put on any football equipment before. To be honest, my first year of playing ball was really rough. I wasn't used to the physicality of the sport. And the burden of balancing time between schoolwork and sports was new to me.

I played offensive guard and running back on the B team. The B team was the collection of players who did not start or get enough playing time. I played lineman to get me used to contact as well as running back because I was faster than most kids my age. My first season, I did not play a lot, but there were two instances that I still cherish from that timeframe. Both were learning experiences and helped shaped my football career. Firstly, there was a B team game after the A team played earlier that morning. I can remember it being a cold Saturday afternoon later in the season. It was one of those days where you could see your breath in front of you but still be warm enough to have sweat drip off your forehead. I had only played two or three plays during the A team game, so my jersey was still clean. The scrimmage was going back and forth between the players who did not play a lot and players who were not as talented as their peers. I received a handoff and a hole between the right guard and right tackle opened like Moses parting the sea. My eyes got big, my muscles tighten up, and I accelerated through the hole with all the energy I had. I made the strong side linebacker miss and I was running for my life. All of a sudden, *Boom!* I was laying on the ground. I had been tackled by the safety who had an angle on me. The first thing I thought was, "That's it? That's a tackle?" I thought about how close I was to scoring a touchdown. If I could only beat that one guy I would have scored. I learned two things while I got up from the ground. One is that I can do this despite the difficulty I was having learning the plays and how to play appropriately. Through all the adversity of my first season, I finally had a moment where I realized that I could do this. I put the fear behind me and put my heart into the game of football. Secondly, at the end of the season we had made it to the second round of the Pee Wee league playoffs. We were playing the Ellendale Bears. I wasn't playing, but I remember watching from the side lines. Instead of me horse playing with my teammates, I watched the game because I wanted to be out there next year. I started to develop a plan at that very moment. I knew I wanted to be better so I could be on the field. I started to think, "How could I contribute to the team next year? What will the process be for me to be a starter and be a reliable player on the team?" We lost that game, and my first season of football was over, but I remember walking away not feeling defeated but empowered and proud. I had a goal and something to look forward to in the future. I didn't know it at the moment but this was the beginning of me falling in love with the game of football.

THE JOURNEY

A burning desire for your specific passion will take you far in life, but desire alone will not get you through your journey to success. You will have to work…work…and work some more. Not just work, but work hard! You have to train your body to the point where it starts to fail you. **That's when one of the strongest muscles in your body will start to train:** *your brain.* Mental toughness is very vital for your preparation into any career field. Some questions I ask myself on a daily basis are: How will I respond when the pressure is on? What will I need to do to meet deadlines? When failure isn't an option, how will I respond? Training your mind for a sports career or corporate career is essential if you want to be successful. There's a famous quote I heard often during the early stages of my sports career: "If it doesn't kill you, it will make you stronger." Considering the fact that I've put my body through some of the toughest workouts there is, I cannot agree more with the aforementioned quote.

Completing my first season was a big step for me. I had gotten over the fear associated with being inexperienced, small, and possessing a lack of confidence. Next season could not come quick enough, but first I knew I needed to improve my physical and mental abilities. I needed to transform my body so that I could put myself in a position to succeed. I envisioned a new me for next year. I am a very spiritual person. At this time, we were going into a new century. We were leaving the 20th century and going to the 21st. Y2K had a lot of hype on New Year's Eve. I remember some rumors about the power getting cut off and that there would be flying cars in the near future. I laugh now reflecting on some of those ridiculous hoaxes.

My father has a military background but minimum athletic experience. By combining the two, you get a pretty diverse mentality. My father was my first trainer. He bought ankle weights for me to wear to elementary school. I didn't know how much they would help, but it was a relief to get home and take them off. Students would occasionally ask, "Rob, do you wear your ankle weights for a physical problem or to correct your ankles?" I would reply, "No, I am training for my future." I credit my father for the early establishment of my work and training ethics. He instilled in me the desire to get up and grind daily to improve every aspect of my life.

As the upcoming football season approached, I had seven months of planning and training to be prepared. Also, I had a successful second year running track and started to become more of an athlete. Track and field helped tremendously with the success of my athletic career. It kept me in shape during the off season. I was part of the 4x100 and the 4x200 relay teams. We won first place at the 2000 SYS track and field championships. Also, I had won second place in the open 200 meter dash for boys 10-11. So at the age of 10, I was the second fastest ten-year-old in Shelby County, or at least that's how I like to look at it.

Experience is a beautiful thing once you have put the hard work in. To have the confidence that you are in control, and know what to expect, is a very comforting feeling. Experience is having previous knowledge of being in the similar situation and knowing how to react when conflicts arrive.

As I prepared for my second season of playing football, I remember feeling a sense of comfort because I had already played before. I remember what I did the previous year and that specific knowledge helped me tremendously. I had a foundation that I could build on; this foundation was one of the stepping stones of my career.

Under the hot, dry and humid air of the summer afternoons I learned something about myself: how bad I really wanted to have a successful second season. Practices felt like a never-ending gauntlet of fundamental drills, tackling circuits, and running gassers—a conditioning drill that involves one running the sideline back and forth four times.

My BRS football team basically consisted of the same guys who participated in track and field, area baseball teams, and children that lived close enough to the school to see the football signup flier posted in the area. This might have been the closest team I have been on. Also, this team taught me life skills: how to be a teammate, accountable, responsible, and reliable. I still cherish my 2000 BRS football team. It taught me a lot about life at an earlier age.

ROBERT HOGG, JR.

GAME WEEK

Blessings happen when preparation meets opportunity. I had been preparing for nine months for the opportunity to play the game I had fallen in love with. I was starting at running back and corner back. The first game of the season, we played the Bartlett Panthers. They were pretty good and had won numerous championships throughout my SYS career. My immediate family and some of my friends were all going to the game. I was nervous the whole week of school. I went to elementary school with most of the opposing team so we would hype ourselves up with who would win. Have you ever experienced a point in life that felt like a dream; everything fell into place and was so perfect? Well, I have. I replayed the football game over and over the whole week of school. I would day dream in school of the opening kickoff, the weather either sunny or rainy, and the smell of popcorn, barbeque, funnel cakes, and more. In my mind, I was putting on a show, and I wanted to be at my best when I performed.

It was game day. I had been training physically and mentally day in and day out for this moment. The opening kickoff was one of the most surreal and vivid memories of my athletic career. The kicker kicked a line drive football in between Richmond Tooley, who went on to play college football at Tennessee Tech, and myself. We looked at each other, and I really didn't want to pick up the ball. I was so nervous and frightened. I managed to find the courage to pick it up and started running for my life. I passed the first wave, then the second level of the kickoff team. I ran right up the middle. Their coverage team had a hole that was big enough for an 18-wheeler to drive through. I credit my teammates for blocking and making my job very easy. Just Run!! Touchdown!!! First play of the season, opening kickoff, first game starting and I take the opening kickoff to the House. Scoring a touchdown on the very first play caught everyone off guard even myself. I was so surprised when I scored that I was in shock while walking back to the sideline. The sidelines erupted in jubilee, and to see all your love ones cheering for you for something you worked so hard for is one of the most fulfilling moments I've had in my sports career. We won that game by two or three scores I think. I remember having two touchdowns and having three very long runs. When I recall this memory, emotions run through my body; seeing a dream come true is one of the most rewarding feelings ever.

BROWNSVILLE ROAD BRONCOS

I was shocked and astounded that I was this good in my second year of playing football. I didn't think I was going to have this good of game my first season as a starter. I thought I would probably still ride the pine, but after my first game I had transformed into a playmaker overnight on the team. I was someone you can rely on when you need to make a play. We finished that season 10-3, I was awarded Defensive Player of the Year, and Most Improved Player. BRS made it to the 2000 SYS Peewee Championship where we lost to the Millington Trojans. I can't recall the final score, but I remember we couldn't get anything good going. They were just better than us on that day. It's incredibly tough to make it to a football championship, so to come up short is a feeling you really don't get over. You just learn how to deal with it.

For the next four seasons of running track and playing football I developed some great relationships that I still have to this day. We were such a close knit family, and all of the kids' family and supporting cast would pull for the next family who had kids playing.

Without Brownsville Road Broncos I wouldn't be the man I am today. I would not have the discipline, character, integrity, accountability, and pride. These are some of the main skills that I learned during my time at that organization. I encourage youth to get involved with any extracurricular activities.

Discipline is the ability to train yourself to follow a set of rules, or to become obedient. Everyone develops discipline differently; some people are punished for their actions while others obey certain rules through fear. Discipline will take you far in life, and give you self- control. Utilizing it will enable you to make your own decisions instead of following behind your peers.

Character is who you are when no one is looking. Who are you really when you stand in the mirror alone? Are you a quitter, liar, selfish, trifling, and/or weak? I would hope nobody identifies with these characteristics, rather strives to be the best person they can be subsequent to awaking every morning.

Integrity is being noble. Having the ability to be honest will take you far. Being truthful instead of deceptive will motivate individuals to respect you.

Accountability involves being reliable; someone who does not falter when the pressure is on. Having the "juice" is what my close confidants and I call individuals that are clutch and reliable.

Lastly, *pride* is to believe with deep passion for your particular team or organization. Having a strong belief that win, lose, or draw, your team will prevail.

Learning and applying the aforementioned characteristics at an early age enabled me to transform into a leader on and off the field at an early age. My teammates and peers were starting to actually listen when I spoke.

NEW BEGINNINGS

My career with Brownsville Road was over by May 2004 when we moved to Kingsport, TN. Over my six-year tenure playing football and running track for the program, I accomplished a lot of personal and team accolades. I had won team track and field championships, and set personal and relay records at championships meets. The football program had progressed to new heights and became a well-respected entity around the area. We never won the big championships but were a program teams refused to underestimate.

When my family moved from Memphis in the late spring of 2004, I found myself in a similar situation as I was seven years earlier. I did not know anyone except my family. The only word that I can think of to describe my family moving from Memphis to Kingsport is culture shock. For the first time in my life I was out of my comfort zone. I was in a city that was completely different from anything that I knew. It was tougher because my sister was not there for support. She was starting her freshman year in college at Tennessee State University. I had to adapt quickly to a city where I was the minority. It was not common to see my race around the city. For the first time I had to deal with racism, jealousy, hate, and other issues. In order for me to survive, I had to become mentally tough and deal with not knowing any other students and being culturally different from them.

The summer of 2004 was one of the longest seasons of my life. I started a new high school where I did not know anyone, including my new football team. Fortunately, one thing about sports, especially football, is that the game never changes. You might be on the other side of the country, football will always be football. The gridiron is 50 yards wide and 100 yards in length, end zone to end zone. The football is still brown, with laces, and weighs approximately 13 to 15 ounces. The first-down marker is still ten yards away, and you get four plays to advance and get another set of downs.

I remember my first workout which was in June 2004 at Dobyns — Bennett High School. I walked in the weight room and realized I was the only black player on the team. I felt every eye on me, which was very uncomfortable and awkward. Prior to that, I had talked to the head coach of the varsity team but nobody on the freshman and junior varsity teams. I was a deer in the headlights and ready to go back to Memphis. I had to mature. I was here, and I had to make the most of my situation. If you do not learn anything else from this book, that's the most important attribute to comprehend.

We had a decent freshman season. We finished 8-2. Playing sports helped me adjust to life off the field. Football was my escape. Football was where I felt like I was home, back in the streets playing neighborhood 'ball, and not in a forgotten city in rural east Tennessee.

MAKING A NAME FOR MYSELF

I learned at an early age how to conduct myself and to have character. I wasn't really out running wild out of respect for my family and my name. All it takes is one bad decision to tarnish your name as well as your family's reputation. The only thing you really have in this world is your name and your word. If you don't have a name, who are you? Where do you come from? Who do you belong to? Keeping your word is very important because society loves to label things. Everything in society has a label or title. Most people are lazy and despise doing research. If it's easier to go off your label or title instead of doing the research, they would rather go that route. Even though your label, title, or slander might not be true. I protect both my name and my word because it is extremely hard to recover from if it is ever tainted or depreciated.

Nevertheless, my high school experience was enjoyable even though it was not the traditional scenario. After my sophomore and junior years of high school, I would like to think I made a name for myself. I was somebody; not just anybody. Kingsport has approximately 44,000 residents. It has only five exits off the main interstate, and there is a main road that will take you to anywhere in the city. In other words, it's a small town where most people are related, or moved there for work. Everyone knows everyone's business. By my senior year of high school I would like to think I was pretty popular. Most students and families in the area had heard of me and the success I was having in my football career. And other students in the tri-cities (Kingsport, Bristol, and Johnson City) area were starting to become aware of me, as well. This added more pressure. I had to always be aware of your surroundings. I always kept an alert sense when I was out, because word would get back to my parents, coaches, and people who supported me.

The summer before my senior year was going pretty smooth. I had taken all of my major tests and was preparing for both the upcoming season and graduation. My senior season wasn't the best in our historical winning tradition at Dobyns-Bennett High School, which is a premiere school in the state and country. We finished the 2007 season 8-4, and lost in the second round of the playoffs to Farragut High School.

During that season, I learned a lot about football, school and recruiting. With regard to football, I learned the importance of respecting my opponents. We started off the season 1-3, which was considered horrible due to the winning reputation we had acquired over the years. In order for my team to turn it around, we had to believe and take it one game at a time. Around this time, I began the recruiting process for college. Honestly, I did not enjoy it. I use to get mail, emails, phone calls, and text messages from coaches all around the country. They all made promises that made me feel like I was the greatest thing on the planet.

Student athletes, listen! They are doing their job. Their job is to sell you a dream — a dream that could or could not come true. That is why it is vital to make decisions solely off your family and own judgment. Whatever works best for you and your situation will be the best route to go. I had several opportunities to go on visits and meet other college players who I aspired to be. Most gave vague and generic answers, which caused me to ponder if they were truly happy? Also, if they knew what there next plan in life is? Those were my questions and I needed answers before signing any letter of intent.

For my particular situation it seemed like it was always something. I went through a lot of adversity on where I would be spending my next four years attending. All the schools I wanted to attend were not offering me a football scholarship. They would simply display interest and later vanish. I realized that I did not have prototypical size, speed, test scores, etc. Great! So I was labeled, which I mentioned was important to avoid earlier.

The schools I wanted to attend never read the pages to my story; they only read my cover and was not interested. I realized in life, it is not about what skills you actually possess; but about your cover and title, or what you're selling and how much potential someone can profit off of. I am not bitter about my recruiting process. I am just wiser, and at a point where my experience is better off in someone else's possession. I have received a reality check like no other. All the success I have received in my career felt like it was for nothing, since I could not get in the schools of my choice. I noticed how people who supported me began to vanish after I didn't get selected by big name schools. I learned so much in one calendar year about life that it was overwhelming. I was getting pulled in different directions daily and waiting on phone calls to my future. I could not understand how all of the success I had — coming from a good program and having a good upbringing — still could not get me in the school of my choice without paying out of pocket. I learned when you are trying to please people, you will spend your life looking for their approval, but it's more important to look for approval in God, and He will see you through.

I signed with Tusculum College (TC) in Greeneville, TN., which is a Division 2 school in the South Atlantic Conference (SAC). In general, I was there because they offered me the most scholarship money and guaranteed I would play as a freshman. After arriving on campus, I learned that there were hundreds of athletes like me — good athletes who weren't selected out of the ample volume of prospects to go Division 1. Before my first day, I had made up in my mind that I would only stay for a year. TC did not offer the degree of my choice. In all honesty, my high school offered more than TC. However, we were co-champions of the SAC and had one of the better teams in the school history. On the other hand, I did not have the best relationships with my coaches, but I would always cherish my teammates. Some of them I still consider friends to this day, and I will always appreciate meeting their acquaintance.

I would like to highlight some of my varsity career while I attended Dobyns- Bennett High School:

Roll Tribe Roll

My junior year our team went 10-1 and was one of the top football programs in Class 5A (Classification 6A now) in Tennessee. Unfortunately, we lost in the first round of the playoffs to William Blount High School which is in suburbia of Knoxville, TN. However, I was able to reach second team All- Conference defensive back and was in the top five on my team in the categories of tackles, pass break-ups, and interceptions.

In addition, to having a successful junior year on the football field, that spring I was very successful on the track and field team as well. I would like to thank Coach Bob Bingham and Coach Brian Barrett for pushing my teammates and I at practice to compete with the top talent in the state. 4X100 relay, 4X200 relay, open 200m, and long jump were my most successful events during my junior year. My 4x100 and 4x200 relay team and I won Region 1 sectionals and got a berth into the state track and field championships where we placed 8th in the 4x100 and 6th in the

4x200 in the entire state. Very impressive after competing against hundreds of schools.

After a successful junior track and field season, I entered my senior year in the fall of 2007. As I reflect there are two games that stand out to me on a great season. First game of the season against (Bristol) Tennessee High High School, I led my team to a late touchdown that won the game in front of all my friends, family, and school classmates. I played both running back and free safety that game. My stats were: 13 carries, 110 yards, one TD; nine tackles, one tackle for loss, one pass break-up. Secondly, the second round of playoffs we played Farragut High School which is out of suburbia Knoxville. We lost that game and ended my high school career. However, I had the best defensive game of my career. I finished that game with 21 tackles, three tackles for loss, two pass break-ups. I displayed a lot of heart in a losing effort, but the most significant thing I can remember is just being relentless and giving effort. Some accolades of that season I was TSWA (Tennessee State Writers Association) and TSCA (Tennessee State Coaches Associations) All State defensive back, first team All- Big East conference defensive back, Tennessee East vs West All Star Game participants at defensive back.

I was team MVP (Most Valuable Player), and Team Co-Captain, which are two honorable awards to be voted by my high school peers. My success my senior year gave me the opportunity to be enshrined in my high school Wall of Fame, which shows a picture of the athlete, sports, year attended, and accolades of their sports career. I would like to thank Coach Graham Clark, Coach Brian Barrett, Coach Teddy Gaines, Coach Watson, and the entire football staff on helping me obtain the success that I received in high school.

After a spectacular senior football season, and signing my national letter of intent to play college at Tusculum College (NCAA Division II), my senior track and field season was a blur. We returned 3/4th of the relay team from my junior year after Coty (Senesabaugh) left for college. We continued to dominate in the Region 1/ Class AAA track and field classifications. We won most of the 4x100 and 4x200 relay that spring season. At the Sectionals track and field meet we got second in the 4x100 and first in the 4x200 relay. That gave us a berth to the state track and field championships. We did not qualify for the 4x100 relay finals, but we placed 7th in the 4x200 relay in the state. After my track and field season ended I graduated from high school the next day on May 28th.

I would like to highlight some of my varsity career while I attended Middle Tennessee State University:

Blue Raider

After attending Tusculum College in fall 2008, I transferred to MTSU in fall 2009 where I redshirted and was ineligible that fall. Due to NCAA rules/regulations keeping athletes from transferring up in division. During my career, I was able to be a bowl game participant at the Go Daddy bowl game in 2010 in Mobile, Al. As I reflect, two highpoints of my college career happened my senior season. On my 22nd birthday, I had one of my best games of my career against Memphis Tigers in front of my hometown friends, family, and loved ones. I had four tackles, one tackle for loss, and one fumble recovery. I was special teams player of the week that week on my team. However, I sprained my lateral collateral ligament (LCL) that game which put me back four to six weeks due to rehabilitation on my right knee. The following Saturday we upset Georgia Tech University 42-21 which is one of the biggest victories of my career. No one thought we even had a chance; better yet be on the same field as the yellow jackets. Secondly, on senior night my last home football game, I had the opportunity to bring an end to my career with a highlight. The punter punted the ball and it was partially blocked and was recovered by me. I had an opportunity to advance it before getting tackled. The offense was able to score on that drive that helped my team defeat Troy University, a team that we had not beaten in six consecutive seasons. We were able to beat our rivals, and receive the *Battle for the Palladium* trophy.

PART II
College

THE SYSTEM

Student-athletes, your journey from being high school stars who are eager to see the world to polished college professionals who are prepared to take on the real world can potentially warrant two things. On one end, your journey can be very confusing and unclear, similar to a revolving door of ideas, emotions, and fear. Contrarily, you can be focused, strategically plan, and be prepared for any opportunity that presents itself.

My experience in college was simple; it taught me about life. Everything was a test. How I responded was up to me, just like in a sports game when your opponent takes the lead first. How will you respond? Experiences, test, and lessons are all the same. They are only bad if you do not learn from them and continue to make poor decisions.

Life is different. It's a thinking man's game. If you are unable to generate your own ideas and turn those into positive outcomes, you are behind and will be passed up by your competition.

Student-athletes, I'm sharing this information, hopefully, to prepare you for the inevitable challenges that lie ahead. For any student-athlete that opens this book and reads these pages, I hope it finds you at a time in your life where you can receive the truth. We live in a world where the truth is hidden and facades are everywhere. The truth is usually discovered through adversity and experience. You will have to personally go through something to actually believe it and grow from it.

With this book, my goal is to prepare you for the real world after college through discussing helpful experiences and examples (which I wish someone would have shared with me on my journey as a student-athlete). I was not as lucky as some of my peers who come from families and/or have loved ones who had the student-athlete experience. I didn't have anyone in my family to relate to or receive assistance from throughout my journey.

Just for clarification, I am not writing this book to present the impression that all university institutions, teachers, and coaches are evil because that is not true. But what I do want you to understand is that post-secondary institutions are a *business*. It might not look like it but it is true. Some of the elite colleges and universities generate millions or billions of dollars off their student-athlete programs each season. These revenues are what fund campuses' nice amenities, salaries, and general overhead. Division 1 FBS college football earns the most revenue out of all college sports. It is estimated that Division 1 college football brings in 2-4 billions of dollars for each season. Revenue wll keep increasing over the years.

If you do not look at college as a partnership, your mindset is already in a position to fail. Like any good business, you get as much out of the asset and you replace it. Once you replace it, you try to improve the asset to be more efficient and durable than the predecessor. College is the same when it comes to recruiting, future student's enrollment, and retaining faculty and coaches. The more quality assets you have at your institution, the more capital you bring in. So if you can start looking at the institution of your choosing as a business, you will have greater knowledge to help weed out schools that want to get the most out of you secretly. The school of your choosing might seem like gold, but everything that glitters is not gold. That's where you have to research and know what you're getting yourself into. College is not about getting drafted, getting a good job, networking, and enjoying your young adult years. But instead, it's an investment. If you invest in a school, you shall reap the harvest when the season arrives. If not, you will be an asset that is used until obsolete, making you another statistic on the never ending cycle of student athletes attending these university.

I want to cover four main parts about college that I think will be vital and is a necessity for an incoming freshman or current collegiate athlete to be aware of:
- **Research and Information**
- **Partnership**
- **Real world vs College Life**
- **Focus**

Knowledge is power. The more you know, the more you can do for yourself. And a great way to learn more information is by utilizing all of the technology that surrounds us nowadays. Something as simple as using your phone to access the Internet and research something could be significantly beneficial. Instead of using your resources to keep up with other people's lives, utilize them to better your own.

When deciding what college to select, research is extremely important. It is unwise to invest in anything if you haven't analyzed and investigated it. Furthermore, colleges dedicate time to researching each applicant they receive before accepting them. I encourage potential student-athletes to do the same.

Some key factors I looked into before committing and signing my letter of intent was visiting the campus and talking with players, coaches, faculty, and non-athletic students. I did this to get a feel of what I was committing to. I didn't want to simply follow others into an investment that I could dictate the outcome of. Also, I researched the course catalog in my particular major as well as the cost of area residences compared to living on campus. In other words, I wanted to know as much as possible about my investment before I signed a contract and became entitled to uphold the contractual agreements.

Researching your desired school could prevent potential setbacks, delays, and detours in your upcoming future. Crossroads in life are inevitable but you can prevent many life deviations by strategically planning your future and having knowledge of all your investments.

What is a *partnership?* How can a partnership benefit me? Why am I worrying about finding a partner when I am in college alone trying to find me? If you find yourself having these questions, it is a good thing. You are on the right path. I do not have all the answers, but I always try my hardest to be transparent so people can use my experiences and knowledge to better themselves in life.

Any dictionary, encyclopedia, or definition finding tool will mention a partnership as 'an arrangement where similar partners agree to collaborate to advance their mutual interest'. A partner can be a business, school, individual, or organization that collaborates with a similar person or agency to gain an advantage that they could not achieve singlehandedly. Partners come into an agreement with equal risks and opportunities — both have something to lose or benefit from through the agreement.

I looked at college as a partnership. I was not an asset; I was a partner. With me attending a university I was, one, benefiting the school and others I interacted with. And, two, benefiting myself by continuing to grow, learn, and sharpen my skills. If you do not have this mindset, you'll only be valuable for your institution until the next asset is available.

In a partnership, all individuals involved share access to each other's resources. Both benefit each party in the agreement to boost your starting point to new heights. One might ask what resources do I offer or what resources my potential school might offer? This is where your research comes into play. Your interest in the resources your school offers conveys your desire to take advantage of a partnership. By doing so, you have the opportunity to utilize a multitude of the university resources, and also network with faculty, students, coaches, and former players.

What do you have to offer? What makes you a creditable partner? In my opinion, those are easy inquiries. You are the face of the institution. You put a face to the acronym of the college that is on the front of your shirt or sweatshirt. You invest time, money, and sacrifice your personal agenda, all for your dreams to come true. You market your partner on a daily basis when you wear your university letters with pride. So student-athletes, if you can start developing a mindset of your partnership — that your face advertises your partner (the institution) and it specializes in providing helpful resources — then both parties will gain in mutual interest.

Student-athletes, when you begin to develop the above-mentioned mindset, it will make your decision and choice easier. You will be able to determine the risk and assets that accompany your decision more clearly. You'll also be able to establish ways to further your career development through your investment. I am not an accountant or have anything to do with numbers. But it is easier to make a choice after determining what has value and what does not in your life rather than moving solely off of emotions.

While in this partnership you have the opportunity to use your investment at your disposal, everything you dream of, you can become. You will just have to put your mind to it and make the necessary sacrifices to prohibit delays and detours. The task may sound simple but it won't be easy — if life was a cakewalk, we would all have what we wanted without working for it.

The problem is simple: Most student athletes fail to utilize their partner's resources and boast inadequate work-related skills post-graduation. This makes it difficult for them when they finally arrive in the real world. Being enrolled at a university for three-to-five years and still unable to compete with the seasoned professionals is unacceptable to me. It is true they have experience, but experience is trumped by an individual who is knowledgeable and well-prepared. With this book, I hope to open your eyes, enabling you to recognize the resources around you that you have failed to utilize.

The *real world* versus *college* is simple. When you're in college, you and your peers are all at the starting line, preparing for the race after college. You have spent almost four years perfecting your skill and are waiting on your opportunity in professional sports or a career. I hope all who are in college would like to have an opportunity to play professional sports. But to be realistic, there are more prospects than positions. You are competing against thousands of colleges on each level, along with thousands of athletes. It's a numbers game. The numbers just don't add up and it is unwise to put all your eggs in one basket when your investment offers a lot more than one endeavor. This is why it's imperative to have a plan upon graduation. I will discuss how to prepare for life after sports in a more in-depth fashion later in the book. But first, I would like to compare the real world to college life. The real world is uncontrollable, unpredictable, and requires you to think or scheme of a positive impact in your life. College is neither of those. College is more controllable, predictable, and requires you to listen to your teacher and study extensively. But you are not taught to think, but to listen and remember. You study only to remember the answers for multiple choice tests and essay assignments. You're not really taught to think for yourself, rather to contribute to the education system and/or economy. Life lessons that are really essential seem to find its way of being taught in the real world from experience instead of in classrooms. The harsh truth is that there is no way to completely be prepared for life after sports. But there are advantages your educational investment offers that you may have not realized.

A certain level of *focus* is required to be a successful student-athlete. If you just go through the motions or "try to get by," regardless of what you put your mind and heart to, you will probably be unsuccessful. It will take a great deal of sacrifice, focus, perseverance, and dedication to see any results that you desire. College offers a variety of desirable experiences that could blossom into distractions: parties, bad influences, drugs, alcohol, promiscuity, trends, and the list goes on. That is why it's very important to stay focused, jot down a list of goals, and strive aggressively to accomplish them.

Being focused helped me to develop a plan, which led me to establishing a network of resources that expanded past my athletic peers. For example, I was a part of several organizations such as Collegiate 100 Black Men of MTSU; and the student chapters for Home Builders Association of Middle Tennessee and Associated Builders and Contractors of Middle Tennessee. I was inspired to join these organizations because they centered on similar interests and enabled me to develop a more diverse network. I did not want to limit my association to athletes; I wanted to have a broad range of people who I knew. However, being extremely active with organizations can lead to fatigue. Stating this, it's crucial for you to understand that studying, class, and academic performance cannot come second to any organization or extracurricular activities.

So how do you stay calm and in control when you're extremely busy? Time-management. Time is very important for college students, especially student-athletes, because their schedule is crazy. There is *always* something to do. Effective day-to-day scheduling will enable you to maximize the amount of studying and work you complete. Some other benefits from time-management include proper class attendance and attentiveness, more sleep, and better diet.

Everything that is important on your daily schedule needs to be managed and planned. Additional activities should be excluded as much as possible, because more than likely they'll draw you further from your goals and disrupt your schedule. Time-management is the biggest skill I developed while in school. It helped me transform my life from being a student-athlete to a professional in my career. I encourage you to take ten minutes out your day to plan your week. It will help you stay on schedule to accomplish your task and goals.

In addition to time management, it is also important to learn financial management while in college. As a student-athlete, you do not get paid directly but those who are fortunate enough to earn full scholarships typically receive complimentary housing, food, and books. As a result, you're left with the opportunity to budget your refund check, and if you do it wisely, you should be able to sustain yourself throughout the semester. Unfortunately, this is something that's easier said than done. It's extremely difficult because with the late teens/early twenties demographic, more often than not, there are a lot of wants, but not enough means to fully satisfy them. Unless you have time to pick up a part time job (which I did in the off season), it is best to learn how to budget your money. It is smart to be frugal and shop for value and not for brands that are trending at the moment. Also, budgeting is a skill that, if acquired early, could help you mature quicker as well as adjust to the real world when you do start receiving a consistent income.

I struggled a lot as a student-athlete because I did not budget my money well. For the most part, I ate away my money; I would literally go out to eat every day. In retrospect, that was not the smartest thing to do. I eventually learned the art of grocery shopping, which, along with splitting days eating meals in the dining halls, helped me sustain.

I can't stress enough that learning how to manage your money is imperative because nobody else will do it for you. Debt is an issue you do not want to accumulate right out of college. If you're fortunate not to have any student loans, keep it that way and continue to build your net worth. If not, debt could overwhelm you and motivate you to regret attending college in the first place. And not acquiring the skills to budget early on will only hurt you more and more as you age. There's a higher potential of encountering financial hardships like bankruptcy and poor credit.

Stating that, I encourage you to focus on budgeting your money, so you can have a cushion, just in case an emergency presents itself. It would also be wise, if possible, to take an accounting or finance class that explores the importance of budgeting. Accounting might not be your particular interest or major but it will help in the long term. I took Accounting 1000 during summer school (which was a requirement by my major), and it has helped me to make wiser choices with finances ever since. I learned about assets, liabilities, balance sheets, direct income, stock, and much more. It was very informational and tougher than I imagined, but the things I learned during that course have benefited me tremendously over the years.

I encourage not only student-athletes, but the general public, to have control over your finances. Do not let your money rule you; rule your money. Money is only a tool. If used correctly, it can open up many doors for you. But if mismanaged, it can create headaches: An everyday struggle to pay bills, provide for your family, and enjoy a comfortable lifestyle.

NUMBERS DON'T LIE

NCAA Stats Regarding the Probability of competing in sports beyond high school:

Nearly eight million students currently participate in high school athletics in the United States, only 460,000 of them will compete at NCAA schools. And of that group, only a fraction will realize their goal of becoming a professional athlete, according to NCAA.org.

Interesting facts:

The experiences of college athletes who don't go pro and the life lessons they learn along the way will help them as they pursue careers in other fields.

- Student-athletes graduate at higher rates than their peers in the student body, and those rates rise each year.

- According to the latest NCAA data, the likelihood of an NCAA athlete earning a college degree is significantly greater; graduation success rates are 84 percent in Division I, 72 percent in Division II, and 87 percent in Division III.

- **Baseball:**

1. According to NCAA data, more than 480,000 students (482,629) across the nation play baseball during high school. Around 33,000 (33,431) receive the opportunity to play in the NCAA.

2. The overall percentage of students who transition from playing baseball in high school to the NCAA is 6.9 percent.

Worth noting, the percentage of college baseball players that go on to play professionally is 8.6 percent.

- **Football:**

1. More than one million students (1,093,234) play football during high school. However, only 71,000 (71,291) excel to playing for the NCAA. In other words, only 6.5 percent of high school players will get the chance to play at the collegiate level.

2. Of the 71,000 student-athletes playing football in the NCAA, only 1.6 percent will go on to play professionally.

- **Men's Basketball:**

1. Around 541,000 teens play basketball during high school. Only around 18,300 will go on to play in the NCAA.

2. The overall percentage of basketball players that transition from high school to the collegiate level is 3.4 percent. The number of players that go from playing in the NCAA to the pros are a meager 1.2 percent.

- **Women's Basketball:**

1. More than 430,000 females play basketball during high school. Only 16,300 get the opportunity to participant at the collegiate level.

2. The overall percentage of female teens who transition from high school to the NCAA is 3.8 percent. And the amount of NCAA women's basketball players that go on to play professionally is a shocking 0.9 percent.

PART III

ATHLETE TO ATHLETE

Former athletes, athletic personnel, and professionals in athlete development were interviewed by interviewer Louis Goggans and asked a series of questions on how to better prepare student athletes for life sports, amid other inquiries. Following are their responses:

JEREMY KELLEM

Jeremy Kellem, current Arizona Rattlers defensive back (AFL League), and former Middle Tennessee State University free safety (2007-2010) quotes:

The first thing I would tell any athlete is to make sure you do not limit yourself. Athletes so many times think of themselves as one who can only run fast or jump high. They don't view themselves as anything else but an athlete. They struggle seeing themselves being successful in a career away from their playing career. Finding something that they have a passion for away from playing sports is key. They need to discover their passion or interests outside of sports while they are still playing.

Many athletes wait until the tail end of their career or once it's completely over to think about what they may be good at or what they want to do after sports. Athletes neglect their lives outside of sports because they believe they will play forever. Which we all want long athletic careers after high school but even if you play four, eight, twelve or even more years of that sport after high school you only will be in your mid-thirties. You will have to figure out what you will do for the rest of your life. So many college students just take courses that will keep them eligible for their sport. Some choose easy majors that have nothing to do with their interest because they believe they won't need their degree once they go professional in their sport. This is where these athletes are wrong. No matter how long you play your sport you will one day more than likely need your degree to advance in life.

The athletes need to make sure that they have a major and are taking courses that will segue them into what they want to do after they are done playing. The courses will prepare you for your corporate job career. Not only should the athletes take the right courses but while you play your sport you should also strive to go out and get actual experience in the field that you have an interest in. Maybe during your off season you can get a part time job that consist of the things you want to do once you are done playing. This will allow you to have actual work experience so when you do begin your career after sports you would not be going into it blindly but you will at least know what to expect.

I believe there are advantages in preparing for life after the sport while still playing the sport. I will list two. The first one is that you get a head start on your life after sports. When you plan for your life after sports while playing, it allows you to make an easy transition from playing to now being in the corporate world. When you wait until your career is over then you have to start from scratch. You have to try to figure out what your interests are and what jobs you would like to have. This takes time which means that money probably won't be coming in and as a result frustration will arise. If you prepare while you are playing then the moment your career is over you will step right into that new career of yours without missing a beat.

The second advantage of preparing while playing is that more times than not you will have greater opportunities in other careers while you are playing. People like to be involved with people who are currently doing something rather than someone who used to do something.

While playing your sport, you can meet business partners, CEO's, and people in general that can help you get your foot in the door with your next career. When athletes wait until their career is over, they lose some of their relevance and the opportunities they could have gotten while playing may not be available to them once their career is over.

COTY SENESABAUGH

Coty Senesabaugh, former Tennessee Titan cornerback, and former Clemson Tiger cornerback (2008-2012) is now with the Los Angeles Rams

How did you develop a passion for sports?

I developed a passion for sports from my older siblings and cousins. Growing up I was the youngest so I learned how to compete at a high level at a young age. My goal was to be the best one out of my siblings and cousins.

Do you hail from a sports-involved family, or are you the first person in your family to play sports?

As, I stated in the question before I developed a passion for sports in my neighborhood competing with siblings and cousins. My family was very involved in sports. It started with my dad and then trickled down to my brothers and me.

What sports did you play? And what made you decide to pursue football seriously?

Growing up I played basketball, baseball, and football. I quit baseball and continued playing basketball and football all the way through high school. I decided to play football because I realized around the age of 17 that football was my best opportunity to get a division one scholarship.

After getting involved with sports, how difficult was it for you to balance your athletic endeavors with school?

It was never really hard for me to balance between school and athletics because when I was young my mother always made me and my brother do our homework before we could ever go play in the neighborhood. So I learned the pecking order of the two at a young age.

How was your recruiting process coming out of high school? And what did you take away from the experience?

My recruiting process was very fun, I received offers from all the Division 1 FCS (Football Championship Series) programs and I took four official visits. My last official visit was to Clemson, who ended up offering me at the end of the process. The thing I would tell kids going through that process is to enjoy it because you have earned it. It is a privilege not a right.

With your transition from high school to college, how did you manage to balance your course load with sports?

I balanced my school work and football in college by basically applying the foundation my mother taught me as a young child. The toughest part of being a student-athlete is time management. It's all about using your time wisely to get the things done that need be done.

In addition to sports, what opportunities did you look for and/or pursue while in college?

> Only opportunities that I really seized while being in college outside of my sport was getting my degree. If I could go back I would attempt to do some internships. A few of my teammates did internships during the off season but I never ventured into that world.

Were you prepared to pursue a different career after college if you didn't get the opportunity to play professionally?

> I feel I was prepared because I never found my existence in being a football player. Football was always something that I did, never who I was. That is the most important concept to me for young athletes to understand. Give your all in all of your crafts to always give yourself as many options as possible. Life is about connections.

What are some tips or advice you would provide to upcoming student athletes with regard to preparing for life after sports? Lastly, what do you think are some things universities/institutions can implement to help athletes prepare for a career aside from sports following graduation?

> I think the best thing universities can do for athletes is to teach them about taxes, life insurance, 401k plans, investing, etc. We all need preparation for the real world, and I think those would be very vital to prepare for before those plans are actually in motion.

SAMUEL SEAMSTER

Samuel Seamster, current cornerback for the New Orleans Saints and former Middle Tennessee State University cornerback 2009- 2013, quotes:

How did you develop a passion for sports?

It started with watching my dad play college football growing up. From watching him, I kind of developed a passion for the sport, aspiring to be like him. I had a little head start. I had a role model I was watching, growing up. You want to try to be like them. He played for LSU.

How old were you when you were seeing him play?

I was around three or four. I remember being at some of the LSU games. His senior night, we were on the sideline, me and my mom.

What age were you when you started playing sports?

I didn't get to play little league because my dad's work schedule was so busy. I had to sit out little league, hearing all of my friends talk about stuff. I can say I started playing sports when I was in ninth grade in Louisiana. I tried everything going into freshman year down there. I played football. And then I ran track. My ninth grade year, I didn't get too much action in track. And I played basketball as well.

How was it for you, did it click immediately, or did it take some time for you to get it?

It took some time for me to adjust—not playing little league and having a feel for the sport like everyone else. It took me some time to get a feel for what position I should play. My dad played running back in high school. Because I went to the same high school, they automatically put me at running back. But I was tall and slim, and he was more short and stocky. For a running back, being tall is not a good thing because you're an easy target to tackle. They tried me at running back. It went good my freshmen year. I scored the first touchdown at running back for the freshmen team. I had kick returns for touchdowns. It was a good feel. I had a feeling I could play running back, but I knew I was going to outgrow the position and I wanted to get the bulk I needed to play running back.

In Louisiana, I played basketball. I played that more so for fun because all of my friends were playing. I could shoot, but I couldn't really dribble. I was more of a rebounder and tried to get little jump shots in the post. That was about it.

He moved to Tennessee his 10th grade year in high school.

Can you tell me about the transition when you moved to Tennessee?

My dad told me when I got to the age of 15, I could make the decision whether I wanted to stay in Louisiana with him or move to Tennessee with my mom. I decided to go move up there to see if I would like it or whatever.

My stepdad, James Williams, took me out to one of Ooltewah's practices. They said they'd love to have me. I didn't know what position they were going to put me at. When I got there, they put me on the defensive side of the ball, which was new to me because I came from playing offense. But I can say I grew into the position pretty well, playing corner. It took a minute for me to get in there and learn what I need to know at corner.

How was the transition for you to go from running back to cornerback?

At the time, I was really just trying to get on the field and play, so whatever position they felt was a good position for me, that's what I played. I felt like I was an athlete, so I could play any position. I tried out at corner, and I was doing pretty well at practice. And after the first couple of games with JV, it kind of stuck with me, like, 'Maybe I am a defensive player, rather than an offensive player.'

At this point are you solely pursuing football as your athletic interest, or are you involved with other sports, as well?

At the time, they've got me at the track, and then they've got me in basketball, as well. That's when I kind of took off in track as well. My 10th grade, we went to state. We were one of the fastest teams in the state. And going into my junior year in track, that's when we won state in the 4x1 and the 4x2, and I think I placed in the 200. I can't remember what place I came in. I was pretty good. If I wasn't pursuing football, it would be track that I pursued next.

I would assume that things get a lot more serious for you as you progress in your position as cornerback. Can you tell me about some of your highlights at Ooltewah as cornerback?

I had a couple. Maybe, it would have been the playoff game of my senior year. My playoff game my senior year…it was the second round of the playoffs. We were playing a team called Soddy Daisy. That was the game where I had three or four tackles and two interceptions, so that was a big game for me. Matter of fact, I got the first interception on the first drive of defense. When they got the ball, their first drive, they tried to throw it deep on my side, and I got the first interception to start off the game.

At what point did you start thinking, you could be able to play at the collegiate level?

Going into my junior year was when teams really started calling me and saying they liked me. 'You've got a chance to play at this level.' And my head coach was saying the same thing. Teams were coming to the office talking to me. That was going into my junior year, so I was like, "I'm really going to step it up my senior year, and really train over the summer."

During the summer as a kid, you want to just chill with your friends and hangout, but I actually took it seriously. I worked out over the summer with my step dad. We worked out, went to the field, ran hills and did drills. I was taking it serious. Instead of going out and having fun, I worked on trying to get into college. I knew I had the grades to get in, it was just working on the skill I needed to work on so a team would pick me up when I showed what I could do my senior season.

To what do you attribute your discipline as a teen?

It was pretty hard because my friends would be like, 'Let's go do this,' but my stepdad would be like, 'You remember you said you wanted to go to the field today.' It was either I had to get up early in the morning, go do my workouts and go hangout later. Or if I was going to wait 'til later to do my workouts, I wasn't going to be able to go chill with my friends. It was pretty difficult, but at the same time, it shows how bad you want it.

You mentioned earlier that you knew your grades were pretty much good. I could imagine your time is limited: you have to work out, practice and play games. How challenging was it for you to balance all of that with school?

I'm not going to say it was easy because after practices—I did basketball, football and track—so it was pretty…as far as basketball, we'd have Thursday night games, and after games you've got homework that's due on Friday. Its like, 'Aww, I'm tired. I don't feel like doing it.' But you've got to do it in order to keep playing. As far as football, that was on Friday night. The practices would go to about…we'd get out of school at 2:15 p.m. The practices would go to about 4 p.m. You don't get home to about five or six. All you want to do is lay down because you're tired from practicing. It just took some discipline to take a shower, sit down, and make sure you do your homework right, but it felt good afterwards.

What was your senior year size in high school?

Senior year, I was 6'1, 180 pounds. My GPA was like a 2.9.

Tell me about taking things to the next level. You mentioned you were getting a lot of interests from universities. What was that jump from high school to college like for you?

I was getting all type of recruitment letters from schools. Tennessee was the first big school that came after me, but after Coach Fulmer left they started to fall back. They brought in Kiffin Jr. and his dad.

MTSU was on me heavy, and Syracuse came at the last moment — like a week or two before signing day. But really after Tennessee started to fall back and said, "You know, we'll offer you a position if one of our other DB's don't sign." To me, I was coming second to another DB. It's kind of like an insult. When they told me that, I was like, 'No, I'm not going to go there.' And then MTSU liked me a lot. I committed to them, and then Syracuse came like a week or two before signing day and was trying to get me to sign to them or whatever. I already had my mind made up. I had already taken my visit to MTSU. I liked it, and I wasn't trying to change at the last moment.

Tell me about making that transition to the collegiate level.

Making the transition, it was different; the level was increased by a notch. You've got different types of coaches. You have to learn the system. I actually played as a true freshman, but I only played on special teams and stuff like that. I actually came in and played as a true freshman. It was good, but I actually got hurt my freshman year. I got hurt in the seventh game of the season. I hurt my knee, and I had to sit out for the rest of the season.

How was the experience for you to have to sit out while your peers are playing?

They were telling me, "Get ready for next year. Get your knee stronger." Coming into the next year, my sophomore year, my knee was still kind of tender. They decided to redshirt me that year to give me another extra year to get my knee stronger and stuff like that.

As you mentioned, making that move to the collegiate level, the level of competition increases significantly. But the academic requirements increase, as well. How was that?

That was tough. It was harder than high school. The athletes had the enhancement center that they could go to, to do their work because they had tutors and stuff for us. I can remember being there to at least nine, until the tutors started to leave. I was in there until it closed, making sure I got all of my work done. It was tough. It took some discipline. It was a rough road coming to the academics in college because you really had to balance. You don't get done with practice until about 6 p.m., then you have like an hour to get some food and then study hall starts at 7 p.m.

What did you decide to major in? Did you have a plan B in mind, or did you think you would be able to play professionally?

I kind of had a plan B in mind. I started off with engineering. I got to the point where I was like, 'Maybe this is not for me.' It was some stuff I really didn't even know of. I thought engineering was you go over a couple of things, and you try to go put it together. But it was much more than what I imagined.

One of my friends was like, 'you like to draw and stuff like that.' I was like, 'Yeah.' And he was like, 'I looked up this class, graphic design. You can draw and help design stuff.' I said, 'That sounds pretty cool,' because I liked to draw a lot. I was pretty good at drawing. I got into that, and I was into that all the way up to a semester before I graduated. I got all the way up to there, getting ready to go try to go forward in the program, I had to turn in my portfolio, and they were like, 'Your portfolio wasn't up to the standard they had.' They were like, I didn't get into the next program they had. If I would have got into the program, I could have graduated with a graphic design degree in the next semester. Since I didn't get to advance in that, I told my academic advisor that I just wanted to graduate with a degree, so she put me in liberal studies so I could graduate with a basic degree. After that, the coaches said since I stayed on track and didn't get in trouble, they would pay for an extra semester while I was training for the pro day. After I graduated with liberal studies, I pursued another degree in nutrition. I got a semester into that before I actually went to the pros.

Tell me about your pro date. How'd that go?

It went good. I was anxious for it the whole time I was training for it. I trained at MT with the weight training coach, Jason Spray. We were just training. We were at it almost every day. I had an all-star game I had to go to first. After my all-star game, the NFLPA [bowl] all-star game, I came back and then I trained. I was ready to train right off the back when I got back. He was like, 'Maybe take two days off to give your body time to recover from the all-star game.' I did that, and then came back, and we were hitting the ground running. We basically trained almost all the way up to pro day. When pro day came, I was ready for everything they had for us.

Would you say you were prepared to pursue a different career after college if you didn't get a chance to play professionally?

I can kind of say I was. After graphic design didn't work out, I started pursuing nutrition. I figured out that I knew what it takes to be a trainer. If I can get the nutritional side of how to eat, what to eat, then I could train somebody. I already knew how to train, it was just I had to learn what a person needed to put into their body to fuel their body, to help them with their training, to get the best results. That's what I was going to pursue afterwards, if I didn't make it to the pros. I was just going to go back and finish my degree in nutrition.

After the pro date, what happened?

After the pro date, we had to wait until the draft. We were still training in-between that. I knew I wasn't an early pick. I knew I was maybe going to be a 5th-7th round pick. I started watching then, but I didn't get picked up. Once you don't get picked up, you have to wait. You have teams that call after the draft to try to sign you as a free agent. After then, my agent said he had over 120 calls for me from teams trying to pick me up. He said it got to the point where his phone had frozen because so many teams were trying to call at once. I had teams calling me, and it was like, 'Let me talk to my agent.' I couldn't get through to him, to talk to him and see what he thought. He had set out a list of what teams he thought were the best fit for me. I decided to go with the Ravens because they only had like four corners at that time. I felt like that was the best fit for me to make the roster because they needed corners. I went through the whole pre-season with them. I did well throughout the pre-season, but they were going to try to sign me to their practice squad.

After the pre-season, before you get signed to the practice squad, they have to wait like 24 hours after they touch you to sign you to their practice squad. Within those 24 hours, another team can pick you up and claim you off waivers to sign you on. That's what Miami did. They claimed me from the Ravens, and I came here. I played in the first two games, and then I got hurt. It kind of started off like my college career. I got hurt the first year there, so they put me on [injured reserve] so I can rehab and come back for next season.

How has the transition been from playing at the collegiate level to playing professionally?

It was a whole other notch, coming up against players who had a different skillset than college players. They were better, faster, and it was a whole different level. You just had to up it a level. It was fun, actually. It was like a dream come true. I'm actually in the NFL. Going through training camp, it was like, 'I'm actually here.' I had some friends who were training so hard for it but they couldn't even get here. I got to this point, so it's like, 'I'm going to try to stay here.' I think I did pretty well because I'm still here now.

With the chances of student-athletes playing professionally being extremely slim, what advice would you provide to student-athletes with regard to preparing for life after college?

It's a slim chance that an athlete will play a sport professionally, so you really want to get into your grades and pursue something that you think you'll like as a career instead of just basing all of your time on, 'Okay, I'm going to do this.' Even though you're going to have to base some time on playing sports, you also want to base some time on what you like to do, so you can pursue that in college.

It's crazy. Training and playing with guys you think are going to make it. I had upperclassmen that I just knew that they were going to make it. And to see them not make it, or to see a couple make it and sooner or later they're not there anymore, it's a cruel reality.

Sports can be there one minute and be gone the next. That's how it is now. Every day in the NFL, you're competing for your job. They bring new people in everyday that are trying to take your job, so you can't relax one day. If you slip up one day, you might be gone the next. You've always got to have what you're going to do after sports ready to go.

Do you think there is some things universities can implement to help athletes prepare for a career aside from sports following graduation?

They have career fairs, but they should make it mandatory so the athletes attend at least two career fairs. Then they can get a feel for what they'll like to do after sports. Have people come in and talk to them about it. Have professionals come in to tell them, "It's a slim chance that you might get to play at the next level, so you really need to be thinking about what you're going to do after sports."

VINCE CARTER

Vince Carter, current shooting guard for Memphis Grizzlies, and former North Carolina Tar Heel shooting guard/ small forward (1995-1998) quotes:

How did you develop a passion for sports? Do you hail from a sports-involved family, or are you the first person in your family to play sports?

I grew up around it. My uncle was a professional player. He played in college and in the NBA briefly so I've always been around sports, as far as basketball. My family members are big sports fans... my mother's a big sports fan so it was always on TV.

What age were you when you began playing sports?

I made my first basket on a regulation goal at two. I didn't believe it either but there is a picture of me in diapers shooting basketballs.

What advice would you share with any aspiring prospects that you feel is extremely significant?

Learn your craft, learn the background. I think that's what a lot of guys don't do but when they do that you tend to understand it and have more of an appreciation for your sport. It makes you want to work harder and you tend to achieve new heights because of it.

The chances of a student playing sports professionally are extremely slim. Considering this, why do you think a lot of student athletes fail to prepare for life after sports?

> I think a lot of kids say "That's it, either I make it in sports or nothing." I come from a family of educators, it's not the same for every kid but I was always taught to have a plan B. I run my basketball camps and that's one of the first things I tell kids, to have a plan B. Sometimes they look at me like, "Why? I'm the best kid on my team or the fastest kid, I'm going to make it." The one thing kids fail to realize is 'Yeah you might be the best in your neighborhood or best in your city or even best in your state, but that doesn't mean you're the best on the other side of the country.' I think kids tend to forget about that. Just in case always have plan B. Regardless if you ever make it in sports, you're only going to play 10 or 12 years, or longer if you're lucky.

Lastly, what do you think are some things universities/institutions can implement to help athletes prepare for a career aside from sports following graduation?

> Career Days and things like that. I remember as a young athlete, I didn't have a choice; I have family that worked in my high school so I had to go to events like that. But a lot of my teammates didn't go and didn't care about it. They all thought they were destined to make it. As far as college is concerned, they need to implement a career day type of event so kids have an understanding and have research on people that were great from their colleges who didn't play long and now are struggling for money. I think that hits home and brings you back to reality.

MIKE CONLEY

Mike Conley, current point guard for Memphis Grizzlies, former Ohio State Buckeyes point guard (2006-2007) quotes:

How did you develop a passion for sports?

I feel like I was born with it. I love sports and anything to do with athletics and it has stuck with me ever since.

After getting involved with sports, how difficult was it for you to balance your athletic endeavors with school? How did you manage to do so?

At times it was difficult, but as long as I had my priorities right and got my schoolwork done then I was able to go do my sports. It made things a lot easier.

How was your recruiting process coming out of high school? And what did you take away from the experience?

The recruiting process was crazy. You had different schools and coaches calling, sending letters and coming to see your games. It was a little nerve-racking, for the most part, because you wanted to put on a good show every time you played. It made you ready for the next stage when a lot more people would be watching.

The chances of a student playing sports professionally are extremely slim. Considering this, why do you think a lot of student athletes fail to prepare for life after sports?

> I think for most pro athletes all they know is sports and athletics. Once you make it and make a little bit of money you think it's going to last forever. It's easy to feel that way. When you're young, you feel invincible. When guys come in to the league, they need to be better prepared and understand how short careers are and how much more of a lifespan you have after it.

What age were you when you began playing sports?

> I've been playing sports since I can remember – I would say three years old.

What advice would you share with any aspiring prospects that you feel is extremely significant?

> The biggest advice I can say is always believe in yourself. Continue to work regardless of the results, how a year may happen, or what people may say about you and what you can and can't do.

ROBERT HOGG, JR.

Robert Hogg, Jr., author and current Project Engineer, former Middle Tennessee State cornerback/free safety (2009-2012), quotes:

How did you develop a passion for sports?

Developing a passion for sports really wasn't a plan. It was more of something to do to escape from the real world; it was something to do for recreation and to stay active. It was things that I and my friends did just to idolize the people on TV and just to compete. Competing was more of the thing than the actual sport, because it didn't matter whether we were playing football, basketball, baseball, or just running to see who was the fastest in the neighborhood, we just wanted to compete so we could have bragging rights.

I was fortunate enough to be All-State in high school football, a State participant in running Track and Field, and also made it to college and went to bowl games. I started to rank myself athletically. And just the whole competing and the teamwork and coming together as a team, that's when the passion starts to come in—when you compete to accomplish one goal, which is to win championships.

You got into it young. Do you come from a sports-related background?

I have two uncles; they played at Howard High School in Chattanooga. Both of my parents were born in Chattanooga,

TN, My parents come from Howard High School who has a rich tradition in football, track and field in the late 50's and 60's. My father ran track and played baseball in Junior High School. My father tried to instill the winning school tradition of football from Howard and Tennessee State University of the 1970's where he attended college before integration consumed the most talented players of that era.

I had an uncle to play linebacker at Lane College in the 1960's and refused a Free Agent tryout with the Dallas Cowboys due to knee injuries in college. I have a 1st cousin who played basketball for Notre Dame High School in Chattanooga, TN during the 1980's. My sister was a cheerleader, and she ran track at her middle school. That's about it. I think I'm the most successful person in my family to play sports. I'm not the first, but I'm the most successful. I made it the furthest in my sports career. I didn't make it professional, but I at least played at the highest level that I could for my abilities.

How old were you when you began playing sports?

I was nine years old. Track and field was the first sport that I played. I was nine, and I was nine when I started playing football. I was nine when I started playing sports. I kind of got a late start. Out in Memphis, there was a sports organization for youth in the different [areas] of Memphis called Shelby U sports. My organization was called Brownsville Road Broncos. [It's an elementary school...the area is in-between Raleigh and Bartlett]. I played with them from '99 to the spring of '04, and then I moved to East Tennessee. That's when I got into high school sports.

What made you decide to pursue football?

Track and field was the first sport I started to participate in. Football, I don't really know why I decided to pursue it. Honestly, I think that was the sport I was best at. I had the abilities: I've always been fast. I've always been quick. I've always been athletic, so it kind of gravitates towards football. Basketball, I'm not that tall. Track, I'm fast, but you have to have endurance. It's a certain type of training, and besides working out, track requires a lot of staying in shape. Football is more of teamwork, and usually I could accomplish more.

When it came to high school, and when it comes to recruiting, I got more attention in football than any other sport that I participated in.

How difficult was it to balance being an athlete with schoolwork?

Starting off, it was very difficult. Before 4th grade, I only went to school. All I did was go to school, come home, play video games and watch TV. In 4th grade, when I started participating in sports, it was pretty difficult because you've got to do homework, and after you do homework, practice usually starts around 4:30-5 p.m.

From fourth grade all the way into my senior year in college, that was my lifestyle. I've always been able to…the older I got, I learned how to manage my time. I developed a work ethic and schedule for myself, which is very important. It takes you far in your life and in your career. If you can manage two things at one time, it helps you multi-task.

Can you touch on your recruiting process coming out of high school?

Recruiting is one of the most stressful things I've ever gone through. I was a good prospect, but at that moment I lacked college size. I wasn't the biggest, but I was athletic. Recruiting is done based on potential because they don't know how you're going to pan out at the next level. Recruiting was actually pretty stressful. I didn't have the ideal schools I wanted to go to like the Georgia Tech and Virginia Techs, which both had good engineering programs for what I wanted to do. They didn't think I was athletically-gifted enough. I remember I sent my recruiting tapes to them, and they wrote me a letter back saying they think I'm a talented athlete, but they don't think I'm athletically-gifted enough to play at their level. At 16, 17 years old, hearing those words from schools you look up to, it's kind of a reality check. Its like, "Okay, my ideal schools are not showing an interest in me. What else can I go to?" That's when the Division FCS schools, the Division two schools started showing interest, and I just had to do what was best for me and my family at that moment. And I actually decided to go with Division two out of high school because they were offering the most scholarship money and giving me the most opportunities to touch the field my freshman year.

Recruiting was pretty difficult, and my only advice is, at the end of the day, you're the one who is going to be in the dorms; you're the one who is going to be on that team; and you're going to be the one with the coaches. Even though it might not be what your friends want, your family wants, it's going to be you at the end of the day who's going to be in that school, in that program. You've got to do what's going to make you happy. You're the one that's going to be wearing that name on your shirt from the school that you're going to. A lot of people I think take advantage of that, and they don't know really what they're getting themselves into. It's an investment.

Can you explain your transition to college and playing for a Division II school?

Tusculum really wasn't that far from my home. At that time, I was living in East Tennessee—Kingsport, Tennessee. Tusculum College is in Greenville, Tennessee…that's roughly an hour at the most away.

It was pretty much the same. It was a very conservative area. Football in East Tennessee, it's a big thing, but the Tusculum program was less than what my high school offered. Dobyns Bennett High School is one of the top programs in the state and area. But Tusculum was giving the most scholarship money, and it's also a private school. Going into Tusculum, I knew the chances of me staying there was slim-to-none. I just wanted to go there so I could get bigger, so I could develop. I was lucky enough to win conference; we beat Carson Newman. We went 8-4. I also participated. I played. I didn't red shirt my freshman year. I got a lot of experience by traveling to away games when other freshmen weren't. I really took advantage of the opportunity to be a student athlete.

The biggest transition was really just being away from my family. I talked to them on the phone. I called them. Staying in touch with them really wasn't as bad as my being four or five, six or seven hours away.

Can you touch on your high school career?

My high school career was very successful. I moved to Kingsport, TN from Memphis in 2004. I was basically a nobody. Nobody knew who I was or where I came from. I was the new guy. Coming from Memphis to Kingsport was a culture shock. Coming to the school, I went to Dobyns-Bennett High School. It's the most winningest football program in the state. I think we're ranked 20th in the nation for most wins. It's a very successful program. They have a rich history in sports, especially the football program.

I basically had to prove myself. As an outsider coming in, coaches didn't know what I would offer to the program. Every day I had to prove myself. I knew what I could do, but nobody else knew what I could do. Freshman year, I started at receiver, corner, free safety, and I played a little bit on kick-off return. I was more of a utility guy, wherever they saw me fit. I also played freshmen basketball. It was okay, but basketball just wasn't my strong point. I also ran track all four years.

[Sophomore year, he played JV. He had the opportunity to sit back and watch how the varsity players prepared for games. Hogg's junior year, he was a starter. He started at free safety. He also played receiver and kick-off returner and punt returner. He was second team all conference defensive back his junior year.]

My senior year of high school, I was an all-state defensive back, free safety…I was all conference free safety…all city free safety. I was also co-captain of the team, MVP…basically, anyway I could win, and I won it my senior year. I also went to state again in track and field. All those accomplishments got me recognized by several schools, but at the time, Tusculum was the best opportunity for me.

In high school, were you a good student?

I felt like I was a really good student. My biggest recognition, I was a Tennessee Virginia Scholar. You had to maintain a 3.0 and take certain classes. I maintained a 3.1 GPA. I was a part of a couple vocational groups. I did a lot of computer-aided design classes, a lot of technical classes. I've always been interested into the design and the computer-aided design. I've always liked to put things together. I've always liked puzzles. I've always liked to know how things work and what can make them work.

Can you touch on making that transition to college and how you had to balance a more intense course load?

> The high school-to-college transition was very difficult, because at that moment, as a freshman, you're not ready for college life. Your mind's not ready. Your body's not ready. You're not financially ready, unless you're blessed with successful parents. You really have the odds against you, and nobody thinks you're really up for it. Coaches think you're still young. The professors are giving you all of this work and assignments, and you're not used to writing this many essays and doing this much homework.
>
> It's very difficult for most people. I think I did a better job of managing my time: I knew there was a time for practice, a time to be social, a time for homework, a time to maybe play video games, a time for recreation, etc.
>
> I've always been good with scheduling my time, which is very good in college. One thing about college is it can be just like high school, but you don't have anybody else to tell you what to do. You have to learn how to manage your time, and that's a big thing. If you don't do your homework and you don't learn your plays, you're not going to play and you're going to flunk out. You can tell the people who struggle with that because they're there your freshman year, and then by your sophomore and junior year, you don't see them anymore. And that translates to the workforce. That translates over to playing sports. That work ethic takes you a long way.

College sports: I was offered a scholarship at Tusculum College. I went there just a year. After my spring game in the offseason, I asked to be released. Tusculum didn't really academically have what I was looking for. I decided that I wanted to do computer science.

[Hogg decided to go to MTSU and try to earn a scholarship playing football.]

I walked onto the program at MT in the fall of 2009. I had to sit out a year, and that's the year we went to the New Orleans bowl. I grew really into that [Division I] football level.

My sports career in college was a rollercoaster: I had a lot of highs, I had a lot of lows. I had a lot of days where I thought, 'Why am I really still playing ball.' And a lot of highs, like, 'I'm glad I stuck this out. It really benefitted me. I experienced a lot. I met all kinds of people from all over the country.' It was a very interesting experience.

Outside of sports, what were you doing in college?

The biggest organization I was a part of was called Collegiate 100 Black Men of Middle Tennessee State. It was a tutoring and mentoring program for young children in the Middle Tennessee area. We went to local elementary schools and volunteered our time. I was heavily involved in that. I was a co- chair for the community service committee in 2011. We gave back to the community and basically served as role models.

I was also a part of ABC of Middle Tennessee (Association of Builders & Contractors). I was a construction management technology major, and it basically gave me an open network for people in college who aspired to be builders and contractors. I was also part of the Homebuilders Association of Middle Tennessee, which is a similar thing, but it's concentrated more toward residential building of houses. Those were the three main organizations I was a part of.

I also volunteered with Habitat for Humanity. I would go out and help build houses and get more experience that I didn't really have, because I played sports, and I didn't really have time to do an internship or do anything but play football and study for school. It gave me the opportunity to get some kind of hands on experience in my field.

As you reached the end of your college tenure, were you thinking about attempting to pursue a professional career in football?

I knew it would be a slim chance because I didn't have a lot of film. One thing about the NFL is it's really about who you know—you really just need somebody to vouch for you and believe in you, and then you need to have a lot of proof that you can make plays, especially if you go to a big school. You need a lot of film and you need prototypical size. I didn't have either. I knew that right there was hurting my chances, but I still had the opportunity to have a pro day. On my pro day, it really wasn't my best workout. I didn't have my best workout day. The NFL— that opportunity just didn't happen.

I had three other tryouts with CFL teams. I had an agent, and it basically just didn't work out. I gave football all the way to that August, after I graduated. I graduated December 2012, and I gave football a chance all the way to that August. I could have kept pursuing, but the more I kept pursuing, I felt like I was losing time with what I went to school for. Once I graduated, I trained to be a professional athlete. It didn't work out, so I went to plan B.

What was your plan B?

Plan B was basically to use my degree. I've always wanted to be a contractor. I've always wanted to build buildings, remodel buildings, renovate buildings…I'm not sure where that came from. I just know when I was younger, I've always liked to design things and put things together. From those two interests, I looked at what can I do career-wise that lets me design and put things together.

It didn't really just workout right out of college. I didn't have a lot of experience. I went to a lot of interviews. It really took me over a year and a half to get a job in my field. I was really out of college. I was working at a truck warehouse called Johnson Controls, Inc., and we basically built truck seats for the Nissan plant in Smyrna. I did that for a year and a half, and I hated it every single day, because I was overqualified for the job. And I remember seeing all of my peers getting jobs in their field and moving on with their lives. And I felt like I was still stuck on zero, doing the same routine: building truck seats on an assembly line all day every day. I'd come home and my hands would be aching. I'd stand up eight-to-10 hours. All I could think about was, "I didn't go to school for about four-and-a-half years to be screwing in DVD players in the back of truck seats and putting them on the assembly line."

I couldn't stand it, but it was a job. My mom used to always tell me, "Even though you don't like it, it humbles you every day. You know what you do not want to go through, and that gives you more ambition and more drive to accomplish what you want to accomplish in your future."

I was lucky enough after a year-and-a-half of persistence and staying dedicated and going through the grind…that's basically what it was…everyday was a grind. I was tired. I was aching. And lucky enough, I found another opportunity.

My current situation: Right now, I live in Pembroke Pines. It's in Broward [County]. I'm a Project Engineer at T&G Constructors, where I basically do administration management scheduling for all sizes of our projects. Our company ranges between $10- and 50-to-60-million-dollar construction jobs from small retail to hotels, school systems, hospitals, banks…basically a lot commercial [businesses]. We really don't focus on a lot of residential work. We also do a lot ground-up projects, a lot of resorts. And I guess you could say vacation destinations, which has been one of my big interests.

I've always wanted to be in a good weather and good climate to do work. One thing about construction, if the weather's bad, you're not going to be out there working, and you're not getting paid. It's always been a strategy to be in one of those markets where you can work year-round.

I decided to take a leap of faith. I didn't really think about all of the risks. I knew there were a lot of risks involved, but my future, in my opinion, was too bright to be held down by the risks that I was thinking about. By taking a leap of faith and putting everything in God's hands, and praying about the situation…I planned for it for at least seven months. I saved my money up. I lived with my sister. I stayed on her couch. I basically just grinded for it.

It was tough. I got the opportunity in April to move from Tennessee to Florida. And as soon as I got to Florida, every single day I was relentless in the pursuit of what I wanted. I didn't really want to settle for anything. I didn't even have a job. I was homeless. I stayed at one of my friend's house. In order to accomplish what you want, you can't stay in your comfort zone. You can't try to follow the norm, follow the trends. You've got to step outside your comfort zone and attack the new opportunities and the fears and risks you have head-on. That's the only way that you're going to be successful and be happy.

What are some things you think universities could implement to help athletes prepare for life after sports?

Universities have a lot of career development centers, which is very important for student-athletes. At Middle Tennessee State, they had resume building. They might have people to come by to speak to the students about how important it is, but I think workshops are something that we didn't really have a lot of…having workshops basically on how to conduct yourself in an interview, how to become professionally ready.

In their enhancement centers, I think every university has a center where they have tutors…I think it's important for every student-athlete; it should be a requirement for them to have an internship before they graduate. I know how competitive college sports is, but at least two months out of the year…I think at least two months they need to have an internship, just so they know, Okay, I have this internship. I know what this will be like once I graduate. If you don't know what you're walking into, the odds are not in your favor. I think schools should have mandatory internships just so student-athletes should have those opportunities, even though they're competing against other students who don't play sports. That's a difficult situation.

Mandatory career fairs to go to. The universities know everybody's not going to play professional sports, so they need to really make it mandatory for student-athletes to go to these events. If the universities and the coaches don't make them, what are they really saying about how much they care for the students? Obviously, they're going to make money off them from the games and off their jerseys and programs and whatnot. But if they really truly care about the student-athletes, they'll care about them after their sports career is over at the school. I think a lot of programs really take that for granted. They just use students for what they can do, and once they're out the door, they're out the door. They don't really care about them. I think the universities should take professional development serious. It should be really right up there with when it comes to training for the NFL or NBA or MLB or women's soccer or softball or whatever. Right up there with it, there should be career fairs, internships, how to connect yourselves in interviews, etc. I think each university should have a professional development or business development person strictly for all the student-athletes, who they should meet with, especially when they get toward the end of the career in college…their junior and senior year. They should have somebody to come to when they have those questions about what they should be doing to better themselves. Those are the main three things: mandatory interviews, mandatory career fairs, and having a professional, business developer for student-athletes, so they can help the student-athletes develop as a young professional in their particular field.

ROBERT HOGG, JR.

FRANCES MAKABU

France Makabu, current graduate student at Western Kentucky, and track and field triple jumper. Former Middle Tennessee State university triple jumper (2010-2013) quotes:

How did you develop a passion for sports?

I developed a passion for Track & Field at a very young age. I won my city's annual "elementary schools cross country race" two years in a row and one of my teachers encouraged my parents to let me join a track club. I have been in love with Track and Field ever since.

Do you hail from a sports-involved family, or are you the first person in your family to play sports?

I was the first in my family to play sports. With time, my siblings and cousins were encouraged to also play sports in order to get the opportunity to challenge themselves in a different way.

What age were you when you began playing sports?

Apart from PE classes, I joined a track club at age 11.

What sports did you play? And what made you decide to pursue track and field seriously?

Besides track, I was very good at handball and I never missed an opportunity to play. I decided to stick with track and field because I liked the individuality of the sport: win or lose, it's all you. With a team sport you can be the best player and score all you want but if your team as a whole is not that good you will not win championships and that's what I was going for.

After getting involved with sports, how difficult was it for you to balance your athletic endeavors with school?

It was not too bad in elementary, middle and high school. I would just ride the bus to the stadium after school, get my practice in, and ride the bus back.

How did you manage to do so?

My teachers used to give us homework about a week before it was due. I always tried to do as much as possible over the weekend, that way I will not have to worry about doing much homework on school days.

How was your recruiting process coming out of high school? And what did you take away from the experience?

I started receiving emails and phone calls from American coaches at the end of my junior year. One coach actually came all the way to France to visit me and I was so excited and determined to go that I didn't even apply for university in France.

What advice would you share with any aspiring prospects that you feel is extremely significant?

I would advise aspiring prospects to do their research before signing with a school. I was so excited that I overlooked the fact that not all the schools and programs offer the same college athlete experience.

With your transition from high school to college, how did you manage to balance your course load with sports?

Once in college, I didn't change my studying habits. I still did the bulk of the homework over the weekend and kept smaller assignments for weekdays.

In addition to sports, what opportunities did you look for and/or pursue while in college?

While in college, I pursued a lot of networking opportunities. Indeed, all I was thinking about was having the biggest network by the time I graduate college. I went to all the free food events, all the games, all the bible studies, joined the chemistry society, joined a sorority, ran for homecoming queen, joined ENACTUS, did community service and I met hundreds of people.

Were you prepared to pursue a different career after college if you didn't get the opportunity to play professionally?

I was definitely preparing to pursue a professional career in business in case I didn't get the opportunity to play professionally. I was hoping that someone would know someone who knows someone who needs an employee. My parents always told me that I would not be able to run track for the rest of my life and that I needed to make good grades and get those degrees to make sure I am prepared for the worst. I never liked hearing that, but I listened.

What are some tips or advice you would provide to upcoming student athletes with regard to preparing for life after sports?

1. Keep in mind that there is a life after sports. Some people forget about this and find themselves lost and unprepared when it comes the time to start another chapter.

2. There are many opportunities out there. You could pursue a career in sports or in anything you want to. Just go for it.

3. Remember that people, your friends, and family love you for you and your personality. They will still love you and be proud of you if you do not go pro.

The chances of a student playing sports professionally is extremely slim. Considering this, why do you think a lot of student athletes fail to prepare for life after sports?

I think athletes are so dedicated in their sports that they believe that once you start making plans for another path you are no longer putting 100% in your sport. Thus, they bypass all types of preparation to stay focused on their athletic goals.

Lastly, what do you think are some things universities/institutions can implement to help athletes prepare for a career aside from sports following graduation?

Institutions should plan some mandatory and repetitive one on one time between professionals and student - athletes to discuss all their post collegiate goals. Seeing signs in study hall and across campus is not enough to grab the attention of a student- athlete who is 100 % working towards going pro and just that.

LESLIE CIKRA

Leslie Cikra, current Seongnam Korea Expressway Hi-Pass volleyball player, and former Tennessee Lady Volunteer (2009-2013) quotes:

How'd you get introduced to sports?

I was always kind of gangly and super tall and kind of got thrown into things when I was young just because my parents were both athletic. My dad played at the University of Virginia football and my mom played basketball at a small Division 1 school. I started playing volleyball pretty competitively when I was 14 or 15. Things kind of ramped up as I got older. I realized that it was going to kind of give me an opportunity to get a scholarship to go to school. I kept pursuing volleyball; I kind of pushed basketball to the wayside and really focused on volleyball. That took me to the University of Tennessee. Everything I learned in high school kind of carried over. You go out of high school, you're the best player, and then you're surrounded by all athletes, who all were the best players in high school. It gives you a chance to keep developing and keep growing as a person and athlete. I ended up continuing my career into professional volleyball after I graduated from school, too.

Was volleyball the first sport you experimented with?

I played basketball first. I didn't start playing volleyball…I never had played volleyball until seventh grade. I started playing basketball in third or fourth grade. It was nothing too intense but I was definitely playing young.

Was this recreationally or for your school?

My school team organized leagues young. And then I was on the seventh and eighth grade volleyball team. And then high school, I played basketball my freshman year. And then played volleyball all four years. I didn't start really competitive volleyball until I was a freshman in high school—I started playing for a club, a local club team, separate from my school. We travelled all over the states playing in tournaments and stuff like that.

What were the names of these schools where you played volleyball?

I went to Chagrin Falls high school. And then I played for a club called Renaissance Volleyball Club.

What about your elementary and middle school years?

That was Chagrin Falls, also. It was in Chagrin Falls, Ohio.

Do a lot of athletes hail from that area?

No. It was a small Division 3 high school. Basically a private high school…like, very small in size. I had 150 kids that I graduated with in my class. I was the first player to go to a big Division 1 school since a football player that went to Ohio State maybe four or five years before me named Brian Robiskie, who I think is still playing in the NFL and then Sean McHugh, who played for the Pittsburgh Steelers. He also went to my high school. We did not produce athletes. It was definitely a different experience because I played in high school, and that was kind of just expected. But I really got recruited from my club team. We were nationally recognized, and I was the 11th ranked recruit in my class in volleyball when I was a senior.

What is your current size?

I am 6'4. I was probably 5'8 or 5'9 when I was 13 in seventh grade, and just kind of kept growing.

Since you started with basketball, what kind of piqued your interest about volleyball?

My family is a huge basketball family. My parents just kind of introduced me to basketball right away. I was always shooting hoops in my backyard. I'm not really sure what piqued my interest about volleyball. I remember before I really started playing, like in any sort of league or on a team, I found a volleyball somewhere and would always bounce the ball off my house. I just remember liking it. It was sort of a different team dynamic than basketball: Really fun, high energy, and a really cohesive team environment. In basketball you can kind of get away with ignoring a player, but in volleyball everybody has to touch the ball. It's hard to be on the court and not be really interacting and playing.

At what point after you started playing volleyball did you realize, "Hey, this is something that I can really pursue as a career?"

I honestly did not know that it was going to be a career until my junior or senior year of college. I was a finance major, so I graduated with a finance degree. I didn't really expect to go into that field right away but wasn't sure of what opportunities laid ahead for me when it came to volleyball. I basically got recruited out of college by agencies who represent me. When I started getting information from people, that was how I kind of learned that I had opportunities after college to continue my career.

Similar to sports like basketball and football, are there actual positions with volleyball?

Yes, there are positions. I was primarily an opposite hitter, like, hitting and blocking specialist. That is also kind of what I do in the professional realm, too. I am the same position, I just play a little bit more in the professional world.

You got started playing volleyball recreationally in middle school, but you actually played on a team in high school. Can you tell me about that transition and the initial experience?

I actually started getting recruited my freshman year very heavily. I knew by then that I was pretty much going to have a full-ride. I switched clubs my freshman year. The club level was much higher and really allowed me to elevate things. I was recruited…people were shocked when I committed my sophomore year in high school to go to school at Tennessee. But they recruit on height and potential, and I had both, and people knew that I was really high-energy. I decided to quit basketball after my freshman season because I really wanted to focus on volleyball and get in the gym. Volleyball was definitely what I wanted to do, and I liked it better anyway.

At the high school level, how was it balancing academics with an athletic career?

It was not as intensive as when you get to college. I never really had a problem. I just had to organize, make sure homework was done before practice. It did get hard sometimes. On weekends, I would be travelling, or I would have to take off four or five days of school to go fly to Las Vegas or somewhere for a volleyball tournament. That got tough, but it's just kind of a matter of learning time management and staying on top of stuff and trying to get ahead when I could. Those skills carried over into college, for sure, because in college you can't waste any time. It's much more demanding, so you have to be able to do both efficiently.

Would you consider yourself a pretty good student in high school?

I was a great student. I probably got, like, a 3.8, 3.9 in high school. I know I didn't have a 4.0. It was close enough. In college, I graduated with a 3.1 from the business school. You have to adapt. There's obviously athletes that do struggle with it—having the athletics and the academics.

But the University of Tennessee had so many resources for us that they made it pretty much impossible to fail if you were willing to try.

Can you reflect on making the transition from high school to college? I know you mentioned you got offered a full ride.

I got the offer my sophomore year and was itching to go to college by the time I was ready to go because most kids don't decide where they're going to school until their junior or senior year. I was really looking forward to it for a long time and really excited to get down to campus and get started. And it was awesome.

As a freshman going into a Division 1 program where everybody has been strength training for a year longer than you have, everyone's good, so you really have to earn your keep. That's not something I necessarily had to do in high school because I was always a really great athlete, and compared to the talent around me, I really was at least up to par if not higher. Not that I had any catching up to do when I went to college, but the strength training program is different. I was so thin, and I got a lot stronger. My first season, I started as a freshman. I started all four years at Tennessee. I fit in pretty well and was able to adapt pretty quickly to the style of play, and everybody around me was so supportive. It was a really awesome experience.

Why decide to attend Tennessee in particular if you were being recruited by schools across the nation?

I'm originally from Cleveland, Ohio, so I wanted to be at a place that I could really further my volleyball career and get better, and not just maintain and be the best. I wanted to be a little fish in a big pond. Instead of being a big fish, I wanted to be surrounded by big fish so I could get better.

Tennessee was the first school to make an offer. I had an offer from Florida State, too, at the same time. And my mom actually is a huge basketball fan, and she was like, "You have to go visit Tennessee because of Pat Summitt." And I didn't really understand what she had done for women sports at the time. My mom came down with me, and we went on a visit. Something that really differentiated Tennessee for me, from any other school, was the Lady Volunteers program. The University of Tennessee, at the time, was one of the only separate women's and men's athletic departments in the country. And that was the biggest differentiating factor for me. I knew that I couldn't get that anywhere else. It meant that we didn't have to wait for the football team to get out of the weight room so we could get in the weight room. We had priority. We had our own resources, and we didn't have to share or come second to a sport that made more money than us. That really made a huge difference for me.

Was it a culture shock for you migrating from Ohio to Tennessee?

It was definitely a little bit different, a little bit slower pace of life. People are definitely more polite down south but I adjusted pretty easily. I had awesome roommates and awesome teammates from all over the country. Even though Tennessee has a pretty high rate of students being in-state, it never felt like that.

How was it balancing collegiate sports with academics?

It really wasn't much different for me. Like, really it was just a matter of time management. I think that's one of the most important skills that a student-athlete can have. You have to be committed, and you don't get a chance to skip practice if you have a test the next day. It's not just practice, it's weight lifting, it's training, it's being in the training room to do rehab if you have something that's bugging you—an injury or something. It takes a lot more time, so you really have to be able to balance. Sure, I had some late nights and some super early mornings, but the University of Tennessee has really tremendous resources for their athletes. If you were struggling with a class, we had tutors available all the time. We had people that checked in with us about how we were doing with our classes and stuff like that. Our academic advisors were there for us all the time so if you were struggling, they wanted to right it very quickly before things got worse, and they were really good about doing that.

What advice would you share with aspiring athletes about balancing athletics with an academic course load?

I think time management is a huge thing. And I think something else to remember is, which you see a lot more especially within men's basketball and men's football, the athletes that are more concerned about sports than academics. But you don't go to school to play football or to play volleyball, you go to school to get an education. It was always stressed on us that academics came first, and I think that's something that's really important that is sometime overlooked. Guys will spend, even women, hours looking over a playbook but then they won't open their biology binder. It's important, but it also helps to have a culture at the university that encourages being in class—that says, "This is an expectation. You have to do this." I think that it's important to remember that you're there as students, too. Student comes before athlete.

Would you say you were prepared for a life after sports if you didn't go on to play professionally? Were you comfortable with pursuing another career?

Definitely. I think that being an athlete really prepares you, from so many aspects, to really tackle anything. Whether it's work ethic, determination, trying to elevate yourself amongst your competition, I think being an athlete really gives you an up in the workforce.

If you didn't go on to play professionally, what do you think you would be doing right now?

I do not know. I think that's a big part of the reason why I'm still playing. It's a hard transition, and I don't think it comes easy for anybody unless people have really like a solid plan after they graduate…like they want to be a doctor or something that requires more schooling. I can tell you that I will always, in one way or another, be involved in athletics. I have a finance degree but I will never in my life sit at a desk.

I actually thought in September that I was going to be finished playing professionally, so I had to sit down and be like, "What do I do now?" It's hard because you don't want to have to face that, but you also can't play your sport until you're 60. But I've had some more opportunities to come to light that are going to allow me to continue playing, so I'm going to pursue them. I don't know. Whatever comes next, you network and meet so many people being a student-athlete in college. It opens a lot of doors. Just shaking hands with the right person, meeting the right person, and building those connections. You never know where somebody could help you out down the road.

Can you reflect on your performance during your collegiate years? Any highlights?

We won the Southeast Conference my junior year, which was 2011. I was an honorable mention all-American, first-team all SEC that year. I actually got invited to train with the USA team, the national team has a college branch…I made a tryout and got invited to train. My senior year, we had everybody returning…didn't perform the way we had hoped, but a great following my senior year. I got invited to train with the women's national team, so I was actually training with the Olympic team the summer following my graduation. I had a great career. It was such a fun time at Tennessee. We had 99 wins over the course of my four years; my senior class had 99 wins. That was something that hadn't ever happened before. And we also won the Outright SEC Championship, which hadn't ever happened before either.

Can you tell me about the transition from playing in college to professionally?

Professional for a volleyball player is not the NBA or the NFL, and it requires you to be overseas, unless you play on the beach. And there's really not a lot of money to make on the beach right now, so a lot of players do go overseas just to keep playing.

I graduated in spring of 2013. That August I went to France for 10 months. That was my first professional season. I was there for a long time. It's hard to be away from home. It's not like when you're in the states playing the sport you love. It's far away. There's a huge time change, and the game is different, too. The European game, well, it depends on what country you're in, but the style of volleyball is much less about size and power and who's the biggest and strongest like it is in the states, and much more scrappy and who can make the most shots and who can see the whole court. And a lot of those players are 25 to 35 years old.

After I finished in France, I went back out to California and got a job last September in Greece. I flew out to Greece. The situation in Greece was not like how it was represented: The economy is terrible; the level of play was very low; and I decided after about a week and a half that I was going to come home. I had a 30-hour plane ride/layover there, and another 30-hour plane ride back. It wasn't worth the risk. It really kind of turned things upside down because I had planned to be there for eight months and be playing and see what happens. I didn't know that there was going to be any other opportunities. It's been about six months now since I came back from Greece, and I actually took some time off. And I just got invited to a tryout and a draft for the Korean league at the end of the month. I'm training right now to get ready for that. If I come in top six out of 20 players, I'll get a contract to go to Korea for this upcoming season.

What are some things you think universities could put in place to help athletes prepare for life after sports?

That's a really good question. I feel like we had a lot of resources at Tennessee that were completely overlooked. We had a seminar class on resume building. There were networking events. But all of that stuff was really, in my eyes, kind of blown off by student-athletes. If it was a requirement, you would throw on a business casual outfit and go just because you had to, more so than, like, "This is real life." I think you see that with a lot of athletes. For example, football players who are trying to make a NFL team and aren't being realistic about it instead of really pursuing a career that they could be making an income and building a life for themselves.

I honestly don't know if Tennessee could have done anything more than they did. It really is honestly up to you. But leaving college, people don't always have a realistic expectation of the real world — pursuing a career and doing things the right way and putting money into a retirement plan, savings, and things like that. I think it would be beneficial if they had a class that was directed to things like that, especially for student-athletes. When you're in college, you don't want to think beyond school. But there are also companies like Enterprise or the MCA that hires former student-athletes. And I think those organizations, or even if more organizations did something like that too, that schools were able to partner up with and talk about together, that would help.

ANGEL CASSANDRA NATHAN

Angel Cassandra Nathan, current associate instructor, Hudson and Holland Scholars Indiana University, former assistant director Middle Tennessee State University quotes:

How did you develop a passion for sports?

In high school and college I participated in athlete support services, so working Student-Athlete Enhancement Services was a logical progression. It gave me an opportunity to still be involved in sports, integrating it with my true passion, which was access to higher education.

Do you hail from a sports-involved family, or are you the first person in your family to play sports?

Both of my parents have a competitive spirit. My father played football while enlisted in the Air Force overseas. And my mother was an avid softball player, as she also served in the Air Force. They had a daughter with zero athletic ability but a passion for competition and love for football.

What advice would you share with any aspiring prospects that you feel is extremely significant?

Those interested in collegiate athletics specifically need to gain a better understanding of the business of sports. Gifts and talents will get you a scholarship to play at institutions, an appreciation for the business aspect of sports and realization that although labeled as an amateur endeavor, college athletics is comparable to a corporation that will allow students to take the experiences a lot more seriously. College should be a time for self-exploration and growth, but for a college athlete it is also a valuable opportunity to experience first-hand the influences external pressures can have on a university entity.

In addition to sports, what opportunities should student-athletes look for and/or pursue while in college?

Although sports will deplete a lot of time, I would encourage students to seek out service opportunities that allow them to interact with students that aren't athletes on their campus. It will help them establish a relationship outside of sports with their future alma mater.

Do you think student-athletes are prepared to pursue a different career after college if they didn't get the opportunity to play professionally?

I think the system is set up to foster athletic development. It is the student's responsibility to use the system to obtain an education that will ensure their personal success after athletics.

The chances of a student playing sports professionally are extremely slim. Considering this, why do you think a lot of student-athletes fail to prepare for life after sports?

Students have a lot of voices encouraging their athletic accomplishments and dedication. Along with their own dreams and aspirations that tend to drown out the reality that professional athletics is a dream achieved by few, and for those few, many times, short lived. More voices need to be encouraging, and celebrate academic accomplishments with the vigor they celebrate athletics.

Lastly, what do you think are some things universities/institutions can implement to help athletes prepare for a career aside from sports following graduation?

I am not sure that universities are necessarily the answer. Students have the dream of being professional athletes way before they set foot on the college campus. Programs need to institute at the primary and secondary school having real conversations surrounding truth of sport. If seeds are planted earlier, more students may have a better grasp on the importance of education for their lifetime success.

MORI TAHERIPOUR

Mori Taheripour, educator and consultant, faculty member in the Legal Studies and Business Ethics Department at the Wharton School of the University of Pennsylvania quotes:

How'd the idea come about to start the NFL Business Management and Entrepreneurial Program?

I think it was born out of Troy Vincent's input—it was at least 10 years ago. He thought that it was really important to ensure that players had an opportunity for a successful transition out of their career as professional athletes. It evolved into the different programs that they created: the partnerships with Harvard, Wharton, Stanford, Northwestern—those were the first four. At that time, it was a partnership between the NFL and the Union. They were working together to fund the opportunity.

When did you step into the picture?

I was there when we actually created the program at Wharton. It was 2004 that we started talking about it. I think the first program was 2005. I was with the program since the inception of it. It's hard to say even 10 years ago. Time flies.

What exactly inspired you guys to embrace that program?

Ken Shropshire, who is the director of the Wharton Sports Business Initiative. Ken and Troy had been talking about it for some time. I was one of the co-founders for the Wharton Sports Business Initiative. When we launched the program at Wharton, I was excited to be one of the faculty members in bringing the program to life. We brought in a number of Wharton faculty who taught various modules in the program. All of the core programs, we had different areas of specialization. These were intended to be programs that players could self-select and apply to whatever program was of interest to them. Wharton was a real estate and entrepreneurship focus. We had four programs going on simultaneously with various areas of focus. Some players went through all four. Some players went through a couple of them, depending on their interest. It allowed them to mix up the curriculum and really gain knowledge about different things that were of interest to explore for their post career and transition from the NFL.

Can you touch on the likelihood of student-athletes going pro? Have you guys attacked that in any way?

No, we haven't actually done anything with the NCAA specifically—the collegiate level athletes. But we have worked with the NFL on a high school program. It was a competitive program that a number of high school athletes would apply for. It was funded, supported by the NFL. They would come to Wharton for about three days, and the notion was that, "Here are high school athletes who have excelled both academically and as athletes — boys and girls." What we would do over those three days is talk about all of the things necessary for them to succeed, not just as athletes, but as student-athletes. So, everything from setting goals to thinking about their brand to nutrition…I did a module on philanthropy and giving back and how that impacts their life both on and off the field. The point of the conversation is that, "Yeah, you're student-athletes but not everybody is going to be a professional athlete." So, how do you, thus, take advantage of the days ahead, your college career, to ensure that you have long-term success and it's not just focused on you being an athlete.

For those who do make it professionally, from what I understand, the tenure is not that long. Can you touch on that and the loopholes they have to go through after their career is over to obtain employment?

Should they be so lucky to live out their lifelong dream of being a professional athlete upon either graduating from college, or electing to go pro before they graduated with NFL careers, I think we're still averaging about three and a half years or so. That's not a very long time. It's actually such a small portion of one's life that you think the majority of the life left ahead of them is one that they have to focus on to create a career that basically becomes their livelihood. It's going to keep them thriving for the rest of their life…the most difficult thing is that they have to find something that they can be passionate about and excited about and at the same time, think that they can be good at.

If you think about the number of people who actually make it to become a professional athlete, think about how small those numbers are. You have to be almost remarkable at what you do. You're exceptional in your craft. How do you so quickly find something else that you could replace that with? The truth is you're never going to really replace that. You're never going to get that feel of the locker room again or have fans cheering for you. You know, some do. Some find careers as coaches and front office executives, but for the majority they have to find something else that is going to get them sort of the same amount of satisfaction in their life. That's a challenging thing, and it's hard to find something else that you feel like you're equally good at or that you need to start all over again and explore.

But it's not insurmountable; it's not impossible. It just becomes really hard if the first day you think about the next chapter is the day you're no longer playing. It's like the first time to look for a new job is when you don't have a job. To not have that preparation, to not think about it, [and] to not be prepared for it, that's incredibly difficult.

I think these transition programs, any of them, for any professional athlete, is important because life does change. There is a next chapter. These are people who are goal-driven and used to winning or used to finding a way to win. If they could just translate that into another career, another opportunity, they're actually pretty well trained to be excellent business people, excellent anything, because they work hard. They're resilient. They've learned that they can't stay down. They've got to pick up where they left off and keep moving, even if they've got a loss. That's what most executives know how to do. They've got all the elements; they just need the training and the preparation and planning. And I think if they can get that then they all have the opportunity to have very successful careers ahead of them. You just can't wait until the dates are over to start thinking about it.

After a NFL athlete ends their professional career, they can decide to take advantage of this program offered at Wharton. Can you go a little more in-depth on the methods utilized to help them establish tools for another career? What are some of the approaches you all are taking?

Three-and-a-half years are average. We had rookies in the program, who had been in the NFL for a year, all the way to people who had already retired all the way to mid-level, mid-career folks who were already in the league for eight, nine and ten years. We had them all. We were a business and entrepreneurship and real estate program, so over the course of the time they were at Wharton, they took a variety of different classes. Even though the focus was on real estate and entrepreneurship, we wanted them to know other elements that we thought were important as well. They learned things like negotiations. We had a section on philanthropy. We had a section on working with your financial analyst. We had a class that was really popular — that was identifying scams. These are athletes who anytime people think give money, they come at you with all kinds of business plans and proposals. We had a session that said, "These are some of the things you need to look at to identify whether a business is even worth supporting; here's how you identify a scam; here's all the elements to make for a successful business plan." We had something like that, that was really popular. We had a business law session; we had several sessions where there would be a panel of former players, real estate executives...we had different panels with different focus. Former players would talk about what they were doing now with their careers, how they got there, how to use their networks, what to do, and what not to do. The participants would learn a theory in class, and the real estate folks would talk about sort of the real application of those theories. "This is how we've invested. This is how we've found success. These are the things to avoid." The program was a whole mix of practical, application and theory. It was almost like a four-day mini-MBA kind of thing.

Who were some of the more notable athletes that participated?

We had a bunch of notable ones. We had a variety of players. We had Kevin Mawae. We had Matt Joyce in the program. Drew Brees was in the program—he was still playing for San Diego when he was at Wharton and then got traded and went to New Orleans. We had a lot of stars, which was great. Not because of their stardom but because they were successful NFL players and yet they were still considering what was coming next, which was very impressive.

What type of impact would you say this has had on participants?

I've kept in touch with many. A lot of them have gone through other programs. They were just intellectually curious. They were very aware of their future, and just wanted to continue to become better, so they took advantage of these programs. And I think not just our program, but all of the opportunities, very naturally gave them a variety of different skills. If you got nothing else out of this, you were able to meet various professors, create a new network, and you stopped for a total of four days and thought about what that next chapter was going to look like. If you got nothing else out of the program, it was an amount of time where you got outside of your routine and could put yourself somewhere else that would allow you to start planning and thinking and visualizing the next chapter, then I think that is worth its weight in gold.

And others were very successful. They used the program to the best of their abilities. Vernand Morency, who was at the time playing for the Packers, went through the program a couple times. And I know that he made a lot of great connections with faculty members of Wharton. And he's an exceptional networker anyway. He was very much focused on what the latter part of his career was going to look like as a business person. He took advantage full advantage of his network and kept in touch with people and went to our program more than once but really got all he could out of it. There are those stories, and then there are others that I didn't necessarily hear from, but I know that whenever we see them, they say, 'This is great. I got so much out of it.' Even if you just stop and think and you plan, I think that in itself is great.

What is the typical timeframe of the program?

It's different. Its many iterations of this. At one point, we did four days, almost five. It was almost like a week-long thing. They came up on Monday and left on Friday. Then we did one version of it that was three days, and then they would leave and come back a month later, and do three more days. We did a variety of different versions of this every year that we did it. And we kept improving it, based on evaluations and feedback. But it was also based on our schedules. It had to be sort of post-Super Bowl and then before they got back into working out again. You only have a very small period of time to work with. We just worked with that schedule and just tried different versions to make it appropriate and available to them.

How do people get involved with this program now?

We haven't run the program. Did not run it last year. I don't think we're running it this year. But that doesn't mean nothing else is going on. While the NFL and the Player's Association don't partner with us anymore, the PA does some of their own opportunities for players—transition opportunities. The league itself has a really strong player engagement sort of position. That's grown to be sort of a clearing house of a variety of different positions, programs, and education opportunities for players. There's that broadcasting boot camp. There's a culinary thing that they do. There's a philanthropy thing they do. It's so many programs that they've been able to offer to players that I'm happy to know, regardless of whether we're involved or anybody else is involved, that their players have options and opportunities that they can take advantage and even do it even more specifically tailored to their specific niche. There's a lot that goes on. I would highly suggest that you go to the league site and type in player engagement, and you'll see all of the various programs and opportunities that they have. It's pretty exciting.

[Mori appeared in ESPN Films' 30 for 30: Broke – a documentary about athletes that go broke after their career. https://www.youtube.com/watch?v=TSOAwNSv8EM; http://www. imdb.com/title/tt2318140/]

Is a part of the reason a lot of NFL athletes go broke after their career attributed to lack of education?

We know a lot of athletes, not just NFL players, professional athletes that have financial management issues or challenges once they stop playing professional sports. But quite honestly, we know people who win the lottery that go broke after they've come into a massive amount of wealth. I don't necessarily know if it's because of lack of education. When you're that young and you get that much money, if you are not prepared and well-advised…it's a lot of money for anybody. I don't think you have to be a student-athlete or a random individual, if somebody gives you a ton of money and doesn't tell you anything about how to save, invest, preserve your wealth, then there are dangers there. It becomes very easy to be irresponsible. We hear a lot about the athletes that go broke, and I think anytime that you have more than two people, it's unfortunate. It doesn't have to be the 60 percent that was quoted in the Sports Illustrated article. I think anytime you hand that kind of wealth and fortune to somebody, it would be great if they also had advisors who were trustworthy and had their best interest in mind, but also had the education and the preparation. And you learned how to manage and preserve this wealth.

For NFL players, if you don't have the good fortune of playing for 15 years and you are one of those players that have a very short career, you have a whole lifetime you have to extend that money through, and get a job and work. It's a recipe for disaster if you don't have the preparation. But I don't just think its athletes. I think anybody who does not know how to manage their money and comes across a tremendous amount of wealth, there's a responsibility that goes with it. You need to be prepared for it, and know how to exercise that responsibility. I think we hear a lot of about athletes, but I think if we can continue to do what the NFL does, which is provide them with resources and support, but education and preparation is everything.

Do you think it's important for student-athletes to establish a plan B before they graduate to potentially minimize the likelihood of them struggling after their career is over?

A lot of them do major in something. They graduate with degrees. But I think if you're talking about financial literacy and how to be responsible with your money, I think you should be teaching these kids in high school, if not earlier. I think the earlier you learn that if one day you're able to live out your dream and you do become a professional athlete and you have the ability to make a lot of money, "This is how you manage wealth. This is how you save money. This is how grow your wealth. This is how you preserve your wealth. This is how you balance textbooks." There's no time that's too early. To wait until they're in college is even too late — certainly when they're professional athletes. So, the earlier you get people to know how to manage their finances, the better off they'll be because it becomes part of a routine. It becomes a habit. It becomes something that's just a part of them. And that natural awareness is what's going to protect them.

Was there a certain amount of athletes who were allowed to participate in the program each time it was available? And once they completed the program, were they tested on the material they learned?

No, we didn't test them. They were self-selected. They chose to be in these programs. That alone is success in a lot of ways—that first step. I think that's really important to recognize. I couldn't tell you. We haven't polled them to see who's doing what where. Everybody came in with a different need, and everybody left with a different outcome.

[The amount of people who participated in a given program], I want to say that we never really went over 30-something. It wasn't like 80 people at a time. It was definitely below 40 or so largely because of class size, and we want to ensure that they get sort of individual attention…sort of less is more in that way. That was about the maximum of folks that we would have enrolled in the program, which is not too different from an average Wharton class size. The professors were used to working with that amount of students. We kind of mirrored that in these programs.

Are you familiar with the success rates of participants of the program?

No, because success meant different things for different people. You can't do that. As far as rookie, it's different than somebody who's already retired is different from somebody who's ready to start a business versus somebody who's in mid-career and not thinking about that but just wants to prepare. There's no equitable way of determining what "success" is.

TEDDY GAINES

Teddy Gaines, current East Tennessee State University defensive back coach, former NFL, CFL, and NFL Europe player, former University of Tennessee cornerback (1998-2001) quotes:

How did you develop a passion for sports?

Growing up in Kingsport, TN, I had a bunch of older cousins who were athletic. And God blessed me with some athletic ability. I've been around sports all my life. My dad was an athlete. He didn't have too much of a career, but he enjoyed football, track and field, and basketball. Like I said, I grew up around sports all my life. I had a passion for it. And I didn't come from too much. I didn't have it too hard. As my mom always said, "Somebody has it rougher than you do." I always had dreams of being a professional athlete, like a lot of young men, to help my mother get into a better situation. Money always helps, or that's at least what we think. I was blessed to stay healthy, and I was blessed with a little bit of speed. I enjoyed track and field and football. I got drafted in 2003. It's a blessing to say I got drafted to the San Francisco 49ers. I always wanted to stay around the game, so obviously I got into coaching. I had some good coaches coming up, and I feel like it's my service to try to lead these men in the right direction.

What age were you when you began playing sports?

I would say around five or six. It was flag football and basketball. And then I got into my tackle football later on.

You mentioned being involved with basketball, football, and track. When did you decide to pursue football seriously out of the three?

In Middle School I was a football, track, and basketball guy. That was probably the order of how I felt about the sports. Once I got into high school, I focused on football and track. I had a little bit of speed. We had a good high school coach who led me in the right direction and told me I might have a chance to get my education in college if I get serious about it. Once I got into high school, I had some ambitions to see how far I could take football. I knew I wasn't fast enough to go too far in track and field.

During these years, what schools were you attending in Kingsport?

In elementary school, I went to Abraham Lincoln. My middle school, I went to John Sevier. And then Dobyns-Bennett High School. It's a pretty popular high school. As far as statewide, we're pretty high up in the ranks as far as one of the better all-around schools.

Do you think hailing from school like that raised the bar of your competitiveness?

Oh, yeah. Dobyns-Bennett takes the football seriously. They've always had good football tradition, and we've always had good coaches who pushed us hard. We definitely played against good competition. And it's plenty of other good athletes who came through Dobyns-Bennett with me who pushed me also.

What positions were you playing during high school? Can you share some of the highlights?

I was a defensive back and wide receiver all through high school I caught a few touchdowns. I had a good quarterback throw to me. I played defensive back in high school. I had pretty good speed, so I got the chance to get recruited somewhat heavily coming out of high school as more of a defensive back. But defensive back and wide receiver were my main positions in football.

Did that go for middle school, as well?

Yes, I was more of a defensive back, wide receiver in middle school. The most I've weighed in my football days were between 180 and 185 pounds, and I'm between 5'9 and 5'10.

Tell me about the time period when your mind really starts considering, 'Hey, I can really make a career out of this.' Around what grade was that?

What really got me to start thinking about I would like to be a professional is when I was in high school I was a big college football fan, so I wanted to see if I could get better. And obviously I had professional dreams also, but I knew it was one more step before that. I got to my first college football scholarship offer when I was a junior in high school from Virginia Tech. When I got it, that's when I knew I had a chance to further my career.

Can you tell me about your recruiting experience?

I was recruited. I wouldn't say I was a big-time recruit, but I was recruited decently from schools here in the south and a little bit up north. Mostly, it was Division 1A schools, a few SEC schools, a bunch of ACC schools…I enjoyed it. Like I said, I didn't come from too much. When you think about college football recruitment, some of the schools I named the conference of, they spend a lot of money in recruiting and they take pretty good care of their recruits. I enjoyed that—going to the schools, getting the red carpet treatment. University of Tennessee recruited me pretty hard. Even though Knoxville is just an hour and a half from Kingsport, I wanted to make sure my mom could come see me play.

UT was close to home and at the time, they were doing pretty good. I came in when Peyton Manning left. They were decent then. It was a pretty easy choice. When I first got in there, my true freshman year we won the national championship. It was obviously the right choice.

What did you take away from your recruiting experience?

I enjoyed it. I'm a coach now, and looking back on it, I definitely was blessed and grateful. I was a young high-schooler. I liked to have fun, but I knew right from wrong at that age. I enjoyed myself. I got to meet a lot of other pretty good football players from around the country. Not too many people get to experience that, so I was grateful that I got to see that. To tell you the truth, one of the coaches who recruited me, he's hired me; I'm working for him now. It was a connection that went a long way.

Before you entered college, how was it balancing an athletic career with academics?

It goes back to [the fact that] we had good coaches. Not just on the field, they tried to guide us in the right direction as far as, "At least hit your books, so you'll have a chance to go to college." I don't think they expected any of us to be geniuses, but they wanted us to at least try. I think if you try and ask for help, you can get through it. But I had some pretty good teachers who helped me out. I wasn't the smartest kid, but I wasn't a dummy either. I didn't do too bad in high school, and I made a good score on my ACT, where I didn't have to take it too many times like I see now that I'm a coach. Balancing the academics with sports in high school wasn't too hard for me at all.

How was the transition for you from high school to college?

As far as balancing the sports and the schooling, SEC is a big business. They have plenty of support for the kids. They have plenty of tutors—just as much academic support as they have football support in the program. I was well taken care of. Once again, balancing the football and academics wasn't hard at all, it's just being smart about being a college kid if you know what I mean. That's what can throw you off track. But as far as the support and structure, it wasn't anything better. And obviously, I enjoyed myself, but I didn't stray off too much.

Did you have a plan B? What was your major in college?

I was a History major. I was full-fledge NFL once I got into college. But I always knew in the back of my mind that I wanted to stay close to the game, and I think the closest way to stay to the game is coaching it. But I definitely wanted to be a professional football player. I looked up to a few of my high school coaches, and I kind of wanted to be a coach for a long time. That was my back-up plan. I thought I maybe wanted to be a teacher also, and I liked the subject of History, so a teacher-coach is what I wanted to do if I couldn't play anymore.

What were some of your football highlights in college?

The first time I got there, we ran the tables and won the national championship. We beat Florida State down in the Fiesta Bowl, which was amazing. Coming in there my freshman year, I didn't do too much. I ran down on a couple of special teams, and I believe I got into a couple games on defense. I definitely enjoyed the ride. We had some boys, I'll tell you: Al Wilson, Jamal Lewis, Travis Henry, Tee Martin, and all of them boys. They were on the team, so I got to see some very good players.

The next year, we lost one or two games. We went back to the Fiesta Bowl and lost to Nebraska. That's two BCS bowls in a row. We won the first BCS National Championship in

'98. The bowl games were always a great experience. My junior year would be my first year starting for the Vols. We finished the year with probably three losses. We went after Dallas for the Cotton Bowl, lost to Kansas State in the snow. That's three New Years-Day bowls in a row. And my senior year, I was a starter. I had a pretty good year, not as good as I wanted it to be, but I competed. We finished the year fourth in the country. We lost in the SEC Championship to LSU. This was when Nick Saban was at LSU. They beat us. We had a chance to play Miami in the Rose Bowl for the national championship, but we lost, so we didn't get a chance to go down there. But we went down to Florida to the Citrus Bowl and beat Michigan pretty good. I ended my career with another New Years-Day bowl. It was good times down there.

Outside of sports, did you take advantage of any organizations or work?

I was involved with Parks and Recreation all through my life as a youngster. It's kind of like a little boys club for your neighborhood or housing project. They take you on field trips—somewhat structure for the summer. It's mostly headquartered at your local gym. I was in that my whole time coming up, and then getting a little bit older in high school, that would be my summer job. I'd try to line some little ones up in park and recreation. That's mostly what I was in. To be honest, I didn't work too much coming through high school.

How did the opportunity for you to transition from college football to the NFL come about?

College is a whole other ball game, and professional is whole other ball game from collegiate sports. They're a lot better. I was drafted in the seventh round, 256, by the 49ers. That was one of the proudest and happiest moments of my life. I didn't stay with the 49ers for too long. They cut me in camp, but I got picked up by the Chicago Bears. I moved around a little decent for them. They kept me on their practice squad for a few weeks. And then they shot me out to Dusseldorf, Germany, that's a little development league. It's called NFL Europe. It no longer exists. It's formerly called the World League, too.

I played for the Rhein Fire out there. I lost in the World Bowl. This was maybe '02, '03. More of my professional career was just trying to hang in there. And then I went out to Montreal to try to get on with the Alouettes. They didn't keep me for too long. It was a whole lot tougher to try to make it in the Pro Game.

How long did your professional career last before you decided to transition away from that realm?

Probably two and a half years.

Did you jump right into coaching after your professional career?

I went back and finished school. I finished my degree. I had a few jobs—nothing I wanted to make a career out of. I worked for the city of Knoxville for a little while. I knew I wanted to get into teaching. Once I finished my degree, I wanted to get into teaching and coaching. I got my first coaching job for Webb School in Knoxville. I coached about three years of high school and went down to Cleveland, TN. I then came back up to Kingsport and coached for Dobyns-Bennett high school, where I graduated from.

How challenging was it for you to adapt back to a regular lifestyle from playing professionally?

It wasn't too hard at all. I mean, obviously, any kind of NFL money is better than most jobs, but I didn't make too much money during my team in the NFL. I had to come out and work, and get a job, just like anybody else. I had to adjust, or I wouldn't have been in good shape. I would have been in bad shape.

Can you tell me about your first coaching experience?

It was Webb School of Knoxville. It was good. They had a good program. They were good to me. They were in Knoxville, and they knew I played for the University of Tennessee. I thought I knew the game, but it was a little different coaching it. But I adjusted, and I learned a lot from those guys. It was a good experience.

What was different?

It was a little different from playing it. Now, I was just teaching it. As a coach, you've got to teach the game. That was my first time doing it. I could go out, run around and play the game. But trying to show someone else what to do, and have the patience and be able to communicate with it. It was something I had to get used to, but it was something I wanted to do, so I got better. I learned a lot from the guys that I worked with. It was part of my growing in coaching.

Can you tell me about some of the pros and cons of working with that age realm of athletes?

One of the main differences I've learned between college coaching and high school coaching is you don't get enough time with the kids in high school to really teach them the game. You get a lot of time in college coaching with the guys, and obviously you get a lot more time coaching guys professionally. And one of the pros is you don't have to recruit in high school. And in college coaching, that's the main thing you're doing. That's the most important thing. I always wanted to get into the college game, so I had to work my way through the high school ranks. I was lucky to get a college coaching job.

How'd the transition of you coaching high school to college come about?

My high school coach is a pretty well respected coach, statewide and around the region. He knew some guys, and he understood that I wanted to further my career. He helped me. He made a couple calls, and I got an opportunity to go down to the University of Tennessee — Chattanooga to be an entry level coach and learned how to be a coach. It went well. We weren't as good as we wanted to be, but it was a very good experience.

I learned from some good coaches how to coach college football. It's just a lot more fast-paced than high school coaching.

After the UTC, I went to Brevard College, they're a Division 3 now, but they were Division 2 when I was coaching. They're located in Brevard, North Carolina, a little bit outside of Asheville. I spent three seasons there.

I then went to Maryville, College. It's a Division 3 college outside Knoxville, TN in Maryville, TN. I was hired by a guy who played on my rival high school, but he was a friend of mine. I coach with him now. He hired me when he first got the job. It was a real good experience. We did well that first year. That was one of my better coaching jobs.

I then had the opportunity to go to Tusculum College. We played in the SAC, the South Atlantic Conference, which is in Greenville, TN. I was just there for the spring. Then I got the opportunity to come here in East Tennessee State University, and help start this program. I'm here now, working on my second year.

As a whole, how many years have you been coaching at the collegiate level?

I would say I've been coaching college football for seven years. All-together, including high school, I've been coaching around 10 years.

With you working with so many student-athletes from the high school level and collegiate level, how common is it for you to hear a football player/athlete say they plan on playing professionally?

> I hear it all of the time. I hear it more now than ever. That's the best to dream. Those boys are out there making a lot of money playing the sport they love. I like to hear that, but you've got to really talk to them about getting their education first, because not too many people make it professionally. That's the common phrase, but it's nothing but the truth. If you've got the opportunity to get your education, we all say have a back-up plan, you better get on it. Also, you have to understand your talent. That's hard stuff to make it in the NFL ranks. All professional sports are hard. You've got to work at it. You can't just be talking it. You know the ones that really want to do it, and I try to encourage them that, 'You've got to make sure you're getting your education, and you're out here doing the right things, first and foremost.'

Is it common for you to hear a student-athlete say they're pursuing a career aside from sports?

> Oh, yeah. I've coached Division 2 and Division 3 colleges. That's lower level football, and the talent is not as great. A lot of those boys know that they're not going to be making it professionally. And most of these schools are private schools where you've got to have yourself together academically to get in them anyway. I've heard that a lot. I've coached some pretty intelligent boys who have their head on together who know what they want to do after they

finish school but still has that love of football and want to play the game.

Any tips or advice you would provide to student-athletes out there?

Work just as hard outside of the field as you do on the field. It's possible, and it takes hard work, but at the same time you've got to be out here doing the right thing. It won't matter what you're doing in school or on the field if you're not out here doing the right thing in your social life. You may not get a chance because it's a lot of traps. A lot of traps are hidden, and a lot of our young men are falling into them. You've got to be smart, and you've got to listen to people who are mostly older than you and probably been through it. You can make it, you've just got to work hard.

With you working at the collegiate level, what are some things institutions can implement to help more student-athletes prepare for life after sports following graduation?

With me being a coach, I think you have to make sure you have the right coaches to lead these boys in the right direction. We all want to win, but you also want to develop these young boys into men. Just get the most support and structure as you can. College sports are a privilege. And not everybody gets to play college sports. And with me being a college football coach, you have to make sure you're recruiting the right guys. You have to make sure you get guys in your program who want to do right. None of us are angels, but you just want to try your best to recruit the right guys.

There's plenty of things to be involved with: you have all kind of different organizations. But if you're a college football player, your time is taken so much. And I think that's a good thing for a lot of kids. Looking back on it, it was good for me. You've got so much structure. I've never been in the army, but I would say its a couple steps down from there, as far as your structure and your routine. That keeps a lot of boys in the right direction because they're kept so busy. If you have a lot of time on your hands in college, you can sometimes go in the wrong direction. I would say try to have a schedule and some kind of structure in your younger days, and I think that will help you when you get older.

PART IV

MY ADVICE TO STUDENT ATHLETES

Interviewer Louis Goggans, interviews author Robert Hogg, Jr for additional advise to aspiring student- athletes:

Point 1: Translating your sports experience

Sports teach you a lot about life: teamwork, liability, accountability, and it helps an individual build character. Character is one of the fundamental things about each person. It's like your name. Once you have a name, you're supposed to protect that. You don't want it to be tainted. You don't want anyone to take that away from you because that's one of the only things that you have. You have your name, and you have your word, your bond.

Sports help with the development of building character. It's not a military background but similar. It's a competition. A team comes together to accomplish a goal, and each person of the team has to be accountable to successfully reach the goal.

As athletes, you go through the process of getting better on an everyday basis to become the best as possible. You push yourself on a constant basis to become better than the day you were before, because if you're not getting better, you're getting worse. That's the mentality you have to take into the real world.

We're constantly trying to get better. You cannot become complacent. If you become complacent, you become comfortable. Once you become comfortable, your competition has a leg up on you because they're always trying to outwork you. That's the same mindset you have to take into the workforce because you don't know who your competition is out there. You might have never seen them. They may be in another city, state or country. But just trust me; they're working just as hard to have what you want.

Going back to a sports background, you don't have the opportunity to see each team practice and prepare for a game, but you know how you're going to prepare for a game. In the real world, when you need to pitch that idea for investors or show up to work to be accountable, or provide a presentation…when it comes to providing a service, if you're not pushing yourself to become better on a day-to-day basis, you're setting yourself up to fail.

A sports experience provides all of the essential needs for real-world experience. Student-athletes just have to take those sports experiences and see that they have the vital skills already, but they're just still raw and unpolished for the real-world experience. Recognizing that early provides some confidence going into the real-world. It provided me with confidence. I knew the structure that I've come from—playing sports all the way from eight-years-old to a 22-year-old man. Those are the skills: accountability, reliability, studying my craft, and overseeing the task at hand. It translated over to me going into the construction industry where I could be accountable—I have to supervise and manage my sub-contractors and manage the finances to make sure the schedule is flowing and we're on budget.

If a student-athlete can take their skillset and game preparation mindset into the real-world, if they can go into work on a day-to-day basis with the mindset, 'I have to get better. I have to push myself.' That is ultimately going to help the student-athlete out at the end of the day.

Book Intro/Point 2: Not deterring students from their dreams, rather opening their minds [For book intro: Not trying to deter you from your dreams, just inform you of the value of an education.]

Student-athletes, I'm not here to deter them from their dreams, but I'm here to open your minds up. You're only taught as much as the next person teaches you. If you can think about everybody in the world, and they're only taught by somebody else, you can kind of see a box — you can see that people only speak about or teach what they actually know. You can't really think past what somebody's taught you. That's very difficult, because that's really all you ever know. The innovators and the people who actually invent, they press the envelope to think outside the box.

For example, Bill Gates, thought about computers before anybody else. He was never really taught programming or how to handle computers, but he had the courage and curiosity to keep pushing to find out more and more about computers, to be the best at his craft. That's one thing you have to be aware of going into college as a student athlete.

Your professors and coaches are only going to teach you as much as they know. That's good, but that's they're life. What about your life? You have to go into your classroom and ask questions. They're there to get you better. They're not only there to do their job and get paid. You're there, too. You're on scholarship, or you may be a walk-on and paying your way. The only way for you to get the most out of your college academic experience is to push the envelope, push your teachers, to open their minds up.

Synergy is very important. It's basically the thought process of two individuals to maximize on the ideas and thoughts that are presented. By me writing this book, I'm not here to tell you all of the bad. I'm not here to tell you nightmare stories. I'm only here to tell you the truth: If you open your mind and meditate on what you want to do with your life, meditate on the things that you have passion for and bring joy to you and your family, that's the mindset that you have to have.

After you graduate and it's all said and done, there's not going to be anyone around still cheering you on. At your last game, when the crowd leaves and you walk off the field, win, lose, or draw, it's only you at the end of the day. If you're not pushing yourself to think outside of the box, and think outside more than you're actually being taught, you only become another statistic in the student-athlete well of recruitment. And it's so much opportunity out there, especially in education and college. There's so many opportunities for you to provide stuff and think of new ideas for the next athlete coming up.

We have to look out for ourselves; we know the sacrifices we have to make to become the superior athlete and then to stay afloat in class. It's very important for student-athletes to have the mindset of what my professors and coaches are actually telling me. They're the experts, but at the end of the day, they're only teaching you what they know, and somebody had to teach them. You have the ability to push them to learn more —get more out of them than they get out of you.

Point 3/4: Informing student-athletes to take education seriously and take ultimate advantage of their university

Student-athletes, it's very rare to receive the opportunity to play sports past high school. You're actually in rare numbers. It's tough to get anything free after high school. Nothing is ever given; it's all earned. It's a certain level of respect and humility you have to have to take school seriously because somebody provided you with a scholarship — somebody believed in you. If somebody believes in you, you owe it to them to take it seriously. You have your family behind you; they're rooting you on. You owe it to your family to take education seriously.

You can't just think about yourself because if it wasn't for the people who came before you, you wouldn't be in the situation that you're in. Whether it's your mother, father, brother or sister, you owe it to them for all of their sacrifices—the bills they paid for you, whatever they did just to put you in the situation you're in. That is why education is key. Education provides you with knowledge. Knowledge is power. With you having knowledge, there's nothing anyone can tell you because you know the truth. You research the truth. School provides you the truth. Sports help provide you the truth, and those two essential things, taken into the real-world, after a sports career, will have you leading your cooperation and ready for the next presentation, project, or the next step in whatever your career endeavors are.

Education is very serious. Every day you don't take it seriously, you're being very disrespectful to your family because they put you in that position and you got the opportunity, and you wasted away. You don't want to dishonor your family.

Universities:

Universities offer several advantages. Most of those are spoken on when you first enter the school: Nobody's going to baby you and tell you go to the library, enhancement center, or tutor. At this level, you're a grown man or woman. Nobody's going to baby you. Nobody's going to baby you after you graduate. If you drop out of school, nobody's going to baby you. If you graduate with a bachelors, masters or doctorate, nobody's going to baby you. The ongoing push of you seeking out these advantages is where it all starts. Nobody else will be there.

Most colleges offer enhancement centers. Use those as much as possible; utilize and exhaust those resources. Those are the resources that will take you to the next level. At my college's enhancement center, they had career fairs that gave you a platform to speak to potential employers or business competition and see what the market is. The one thing I failed to do in college is get an internship. I didn't get one, and this hindered my experience after graduation, and it sat me back in the hiring process. I wasn't able to get a job right out of college because couldn't prove that I was experienced. A degree is good nowadays, but a degree and experience is great. Nowadays, you can't settle for being good, you have to be great. You have to have experience and an education. What's somebody who knows everything but fails to know how to do it? And who is somebody who knows how to do everything but doesn't know the smartest way and the safest way?

Employers are getting very smart on their hiring process, and you don't want to be on the outside looking it. Colleges provide excellent advantages and resources for you to take. You just have to research them, seek them out, get the training on whatever requirements for your major, and explore those to the best of your abilities, and it will put you into a position either after a professional career or out of college to be successful. But it starts with you.

Additional info:

In school, I got a lot of opportunities to play ball my senior year, but my freshman through junior year, I just kind of sat back and watched. I've seen a lot of cats come through the program and they either didn't make it…if it's like 40 or 50 dudes at my school [playing football], and it's thousands of schools out there — D1, D2, D3, Junior Colleges, Community College, and NAIA schools. Each have football programs, basketball programs, that's, like, millions of kids. Those are the people going into the workforce. And it's no telling, they probably have other responsibilities, like, a kid, mom and dad not doing well, etc. That's who America really is. The guys who make it in these first-round picks, those are the chosen ones. But the other people, they've got to read this.

I want to hit on what an individual can control for themselves without any exterior help—this is all stuff they can seek out. At the end of the day, that's the answer. You're the answer. You have to get out there and do it. You have to stay up late, pass that test, or study the playbook, just so you can perform whenever your game is.

TAKE CONTROL OF YOUR DESTINY

Student-athletes, whether you're preparing to enter college or about to exit, I hope you're able to gain valuable information from this book. I would like to conclude with the most important section of this book: answers. Up to this point, topics have centered largely on the problems and conflicts associated with being a student-athlete. I'm aware this could potentially discourage, burden, and/or place doubt in you. But please do not misinterpret the things in this book and waver away from your plans to enjoy a bright future. Having all the cards in your hand will help you make more accurate decisions. Instead of making poor choices that could cost you time, effort, energy, and money; you can avoid this by strategically planning your future and leaving designated room for growth and improvement.

Student-athletes, not making it to the pros does not classify you as a failure. Your athletic experience is more than enough to contribute to your success in any interest you have. Learning how to translate your athletic background into a real-world scenario is significant. The same approach you take with life, preparing to be a better athlete, you should utilize in every day life.

As athletes, we dedicate so much of our lives to being the best version of ourselves. I can wholeheartedly say sports have helped me develop more character, integrity, and discipline than anything else I have put my mind to thus far. So take the experiences you learn on the field or court and use them to better your life. Sports are not solely about winning a game: they teach you about life from a mental and physical realm. An athlete goes through numerous trials and tribulations over the course of their career. For example, they suffer injuries that jeopardize not only their athletic career, but they're way of life completely. They also experience a myriad of challenges: coach and player changes, opposing crowds, lengthy traveling, and last minute losses. It can all be viewed negatively, but in retrospect each issue can serve as a learning curve that makes you a better person.

There are several main characteristics that a successful student-athlete should develop while playing, which will translate over to the real world, helping make your transition from student-athlete to professional easier. These same characteristics helped me get through the college system and to the young professional I am today:

- **Faith**
- **Perseverance**
- **Responsible**
- **Confidence**

What is *faith*? For spiritual believers, faith can be considered believing in a higher power that no matter what might happen through the course of your life, the Lord always has your best interest at heart. My personal belief is without faith, you cannot accomplish anything. You have to first believe in yourself; you can accomplish anything you put your heart and mind too. A favorite passage of mine from the Holy Bible (KJV) is Matthew 17:20: *"And Jesus said unto them, Because of your unbelief: for verily I say unto you, If ye have faith as a grain of mustard seed, ye shall say unto this mountain, Remove hence to yonder place; and it shall remove; and nothing shall be impossible unto you."* This passage is popular among many believers. It virtually serves as the foundation of many successful individuals who put their faith into a higher power's hands. By doing so, many blessings will rain down on you. And as you receive your blessings, it is important to empty your cup to the next person, serving as a blessing to them.

Perseverance is required to perfect any talent you were blessed with. My personal belief of perseverance is continuing to seek an accomplishment despite encountering various obstacles during your journey. This accomplishment can be a goal that takes hours to obtain, maybe even decades, or possibly a lifetime. I value this skill because it is what got me through college. Walking on a Division 1 college football team isn't easy, and enduring the grind and multiple setbacks that I encountered wasn't either. But I must admit; experiencing that type of adversity made me a greater man. Having to work your butt off for every bit of opportunity, and at the slightest mistake getting punished, helped me put life into perspective about opportunities, which I learned over the years come and go easily. Student-athletes, you have to be ready for opportunity at all times. If you persevere through your journey, but have not become prepared along the way, you have basically wasted your time and everyone else's who has helped you.

As a man or woman, the more mature you become, the more *responsibilities* you will have to take on. That's just a part of growth. After I began college, I started to prioritize my life more effectively. I started to understand what held value and what didn't. If nothing else, my job was to gain knowledge while in college, and leave school with a better opportunity than I would have without a college degree. It was my responsibility to protect the investment I made in my future, as well as make the most out of the sacrifices my loved ones made to help me get to where I am now. Student-athletes, there is no one else on this planet responsible for how successful you manage to become other than you. Yes, people do provide opportunities, but it's ultimately up to you to take advantage and make the best out of those opportunities. Taking control of your destiny is a responsibility that you must have for yourself; you have to believe with all your heart that you can accomplish your goals.

Finally, **confidence** is a vital characteristic for any athlete. The higher level of playing field you are competing on, the more confidence in your abilities you must possess. Student-athletes, having confidence in yourself basically requires the ability to maintain belief through all odds, obstacles, and setbacks you encounter. On the contrary, too much confidence can be negative and cause other individuals to not like your presence. It is essential to remain humble as well as believe in yourself through any challenge. Many individuals fail to accomplish their goals because they lack confidence. They are defeated before they even take the first step. However, the first step is usually the hardest; you have to take a leap of faith to even get started. But looking back in retrospect, I had a lot of confidence in my abilities and what I could bring to my team. Without faith and confidence in myself, I would have never survived the gauntlet of the college football system.

As I conclude, student-athletes, the answers to your questions lie within your own being. It is imperative to find your purpose in life and pursue that with a burning desire. Your purpose in life is the only thing that will bring you joy. Any other motivation will not be sufficient and could lead to your destruction. Open your mind and be different. It is important not to follow trends or be overly-influenced by your peers. Being a young adult comes with many perks, but it is vital to find and stay true to oneself during an emotional rollercoaster of feelings and challenges, which could detour you from your purpose.

Despite this book providing you with an exclusive insight on what's ahead of you, it is still up to you to make the best decisions. With that being said, I hope and pray you go out and be outstanding individuals in whatever you choose to do. God Bless!!!

SOURCES

Sources of information for the aforementioned information:

- High school figures from the 2013-14 High School Athletics Participation Survey conducted by the National Federation of State High School Associations.

- College numbers from the NCAA 2013-14 Sports Sponsorship and Participation Rates Report.

Probability of competing in sports beyond high school:
http://www.ncaa.org/about/resources/research/probability-competing-beyond-high-school

Estimated probability of competing in college:
http://www.ncaa.org/about/resources/research/estimated-probability-competing-college-athletics

Estimated probability of going pro:
http://www.ncaa.org/sites/default/files/2015%20Probability%20Chart%20Web%20PDF_draft5.pdf